MW00608799

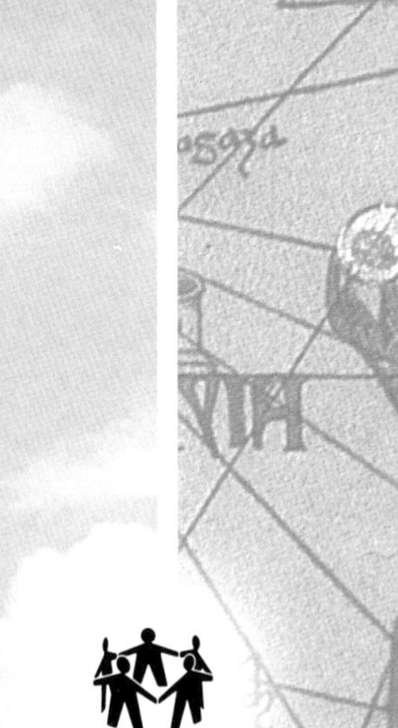
Core Knowledge®

Printed in Canada

ISBN: 978-1-68380-265-5

Medieval Islamic Empires

Table of Contents

Reader

Core Knowledge History and Geography™

Chapter 1
The Pillars of Islam

The Call to Prayer Khalid ibn Zayd climbed the stairs that circled the outside of the tower. It was not an easy climb. It was just after noon, and the sun was beating down on the tower and the buildings below. The city was Cairo, Egypt, and the year was 1082 CE.

The Big Question

Within the religion of Islam, who is Muhammad?

There were 175 steps in all, but Khalid no longer thought to count them. When he reached the top step of the tower, he turned and looked down on the courtyard below. Then, he raised his hands beside his head, palms forward, took a deep breath, and called his neighbors to prayer.

Below him, worshippers moved steadily through doors cut into the courtyard wall. They moved toward a covered area near the opposite wall. Before entering the area, worshippers removed their shoes, covered their heads, and carefully took their places facing a small arch cut into the wall.

Vocabulary

minaret, n. a high tower on a mosque, from which Muslims may be called to prayer

muezzin, n. a religious official who calls Muslims to prayer

High on a minaret, a muezzin calls the Muslim faithful to prayer five times a day. This happens today, just as it did hundreds of years ago.

Like Khalid, they raised their hands beside their heads, palms forward, and prayed in Arabic, *"Allahu Akbar"* ("God is great!")—Allah being the Arabic word for God.

The worshippers then knelt down and bowed their heads to the ground, while praising God for his goodness.

Toward Mecca

Khalid ibn Zayd was proud of the service he performed. He was a *muezzin* (/myoo*ez*ihn/), a special person trained to call others to prayer. Five times a day he climbed the tall tower, known as a minaret, (/mihn*uh*ret/) and called people to prayer.

The worshippers Khalid summoned were Muslims (/muz*lumz/). Muslims follow the religion Islam (/ihs*lahm/), which means "surrendering to God." Muslims, then, are "those who have given themselves to God or His will."

Many Muslims pray in a building called a **mosque** (/mahsk/). Muslims, however, believe prayer can take place anywhere. When they pray, Muslims face toward Mecca, an important city in Islam. Mecca is located on the Arabian Peninsula in the Middle East in present-day Saudi Arabia. For Muslims, Mecca is the holiest city because it is the birthplace of Muhammad, the **prophet** of Islam.

It is also the location of an important religious site called the Kaaba where Muslims perform an annual **pilgrimage** (*hajj*).

Vocabulary

mosque, n. a place of worship for Muslims

prophet, n. someone chosen by God to bring a message to people

pilgrimage (hajj in Arabic), n. a journey undertaken for a religious purpose

Muslims worship in a building called a mosque.

God's Messenger

Khalid ibn Zayd felt fortunate that he lived in Cairo, which was a great center of Islamic learning. There his son, Yusuf, could attend a madrasa (/ma*dra*sah/), or Islamic school. There, Yusuf learned how to read Arabic and how to live according to the Koran, the sacred scripture of Islam.

Soon after the noon prayers, young Yusuf ibn Khalid returned to his schoolroom in the madrasa.

"Peace be upon you," the teacher greeted the students.

"And on you be peace," responded the students in one voice.

"Yusuf," his teacher called, "why do we Muslims worship Muhammad, peace be upon him?"

Yusuf knew it was a trick question.

"Sir," he answered, "we do not worship Muhammad, peace be upon him. We honor him as God's greatest messenger, but we worship God alone."

"Well said," replied the teacher, smiling. "Tell me more about Muhammad. How did he come to be God's messenger?"

"Once, when Muhammad was asleep," Yusuf answered with confidence, "the angel Gabriel came to him in a **vision** and told him to recite a **verse**. He was afraid. As he ran away, he heard the voice of the angel telling him that he was God's messenger."

Vocabulary

vision, n. an image in one's mind or imagination that others cannot see

verse, n. a part of a poem, song, or religious text, such as the Bible, or rhymed prose, such as the Koran

Muslims believe that the angel Gabriel visited Muhammad when he was praying in a cave outside of Mecca.

"And did Muhammad begin immediately to act as God's messenger?" asked the teacher.

"No," said Yusuf, "he was still afraid. But the angel came to him again and again until he began to preach God's message."

"You have listened well, Yusuf," said the teacher. Yusuf bowed slightly and smiled, happy with his teacher's praise.

"Ali," the teacher called to a tall boy seated beside Yusuf, "did the people listen to what Muhammad said?"

"No," replied Ali. "At first only a few people among Muhammad's family and friends believed what he said. Most of the people ignored him or did not accept his message."

"And what did he say that made him unpopular?" prodded the teacher.

"Well," Ali answered thoughtfully, "he told them that there was only one God, Allah. He told them they should not worship other gods or **idols**. The people did not like that because they had lots of gods and put statues of them in the Kaaba."

"And what was the Kaaba?" the teacher cut in.

"It was a **shrine** where various gods and idols were worshipped."

"And what is it today?"

"It is the holiest place in Islam," answered Ali, adding quickly, "and today only God is worshipped there."

Vocabulary

idol, n. an object, such as a statue or carving, that represents a god and is worshipped

shrine, n. a place considered holy because it is associated with a religious person or saint

The Five Pillars of Islam

"Excellent," said the teacher. "We believe only in God the Almighty. That is the first pillar, or foundation, of our faith. We believe there is no lord but God and that Muhammad is the last messenger of God."

"What are the other pillars of our faith?" the teacher asked. "You first, Hassan," he said to a boy sitting nearby.

"The second pillar of our faith," Hassan responded, "is prayer. Five times a day we Muslims pray toward the Kaaba in Mecca. We must pray before the sun rises, after midday, in the afternoon, about sunset, and at night.

"The third pillar," Hassan continued, "is sharing wealth with the poor. It is called *zakat*. Muhammad taught that we must help the poor and those in need by giving them money."

"You have answered well," said the teacher. "Let's give someone else a chance to answer now."

"Ishaq," he called to a boy sitting next to Hassan, "what is the fourth pillar of our faith?"

> **Vocabulary**
>
> **Ramadan,** n. a holy month in the Islamic calendar when Muslims fast from sunrise to sunset

"The fourth pillar is fasting," Ishaq said. "We Muslims fast during the month of **Ramadan**. That means . . . uhm . . . it means that we do not eat or drink between sunrise and sunset for the whole month."

"And the fifth pillar, Ishaq?" encouraged the teacher.

"Well, . . . the fifth pillar," said Ishaq slowly, stalling for time. "The fifth pillar," Ishaq finally said, "is to make a **pilgrimage** to Mecca.

A young Muslim girl reads the Koran, much as the students in the story did almost one thousand years ago.

"If we are able," Ishaq continued, "we should visit Mecca at least once in our lives."

"Well done, Ishaq," said the teacher with genuine pleasure. "You all have answered well today." He was very proud of his students and all they had learned about their faith.

Since the beginning of Islam, Muslim youth have attended their local mosques and later madrasas to learn more about their faith and how to be good Muslims. Today, Islamic schools much like the one described can be found in many parts of the world, such as Egypt, Nigeria, India, France, and the United States.

Chapter 2
Muhammad

Who Was the Prophet? Muhammad was born in the Arabian city of Mecca more than 1,400 years ago, in about 570 CE. Muhammad's father died shortly before he was born. According to Arabian tribal society, when a father dies, a child becomes an orphan, and so Muhammad became an orphan. He was raised by his uncle. Muhammad grew up to become a well-respected trader in his community.

> **The Big Question**
>
> What does Muhammad's decision regarding the replacement of the holy stone reveal about his character?

This tapestry shows the Muslim holy city of Mecca.

Muslims tell a story about Muhammad to show why people respected him. One year, floodwaters badly damaged the Kaaba. The Kaaba is a holy shrine in Mecca that houses a **sacred** black stone. In Muhammad's time, people visited the shrine to worship many different gods. The flood knocked the stone loose from its special place in one of the Kaaba's walls. At that time there were many groups of families, called **clans**, living in Mecca. These clans argued over which one would have the privilege of replacing the stone. They could not agree. They decided that the next man who entered the courtyard would decide.

Vocabulary

sacred, adj. related to religion; holy

clan, n. a group of families claiming a common ancestor

Muhammad was the next man to enter. He found a unique solution. He took off his cloak and spread it on the ground. He placed the sacred stone in the middle of it. Then he invited all of the clan

The black building in the center of this picture is the Kaaba, the holiest place in all of Islam. The Kaaba is in the grand mosque in Mecca.

leaders to take hold of the ends of the cloak. Carefully, they lifted the stone to its place in the wall. Finally, Muhammad gently slid the stone into its place. The clan leaders praised him for his solution to a difficult problem.

Muhammad: The Prophet

Muhammad was a thoughtful man. Often he would go off by himself to reflect on life and how it should be lived. In 610, while **meditating**, Muhammad had a vision. He believed the angel Gabriel, a messenger from God, appeared to him. Gabriel told him he was to be God's messenger. At first, he was confused and frightened. Muhammad did not know what he was expected to do. His wife, some family members, and friends reassured him. They told him he was meant to be a prophet who spoke on behalf of God.

> **Vocabulary**
>
> **meditate,** v. to think quietly or carefully about something

In 613, after a second vision, Muhammad began sharing the messages he received. He said that there was only one God, Allah. People should pray to God alone, he insisted. Muhammad also taught that all believers were equal in God's eyes. The rich, he said, must share their wealth with the poor. He warned people that they would be judged by their actions, not by their wealth.

Some people accepted the messages shared by Muhammad, but many opposed them. People of many faiths came to Mecca to worship their gods at the Kaaba. They spent a lot of money in Mecca. Would these people still come if the people of Mecca started to worship only Allah? Even some members of Muhammad's clan stopped supporting him. He would not have their protection if he were attacked.

A Narrow Escape: The Hegira

Muhammad was worried that he and his followers were not safe in Mecca. Muhammad and his followers were invited by two Arab clans to move to Medina, a town two hundred or so miles north of Mecca. In July 622, Muhammad arranged to have most of his followers leave Mecca. But Mohammad himself remained in Mecca.

The Arabian Peninsula

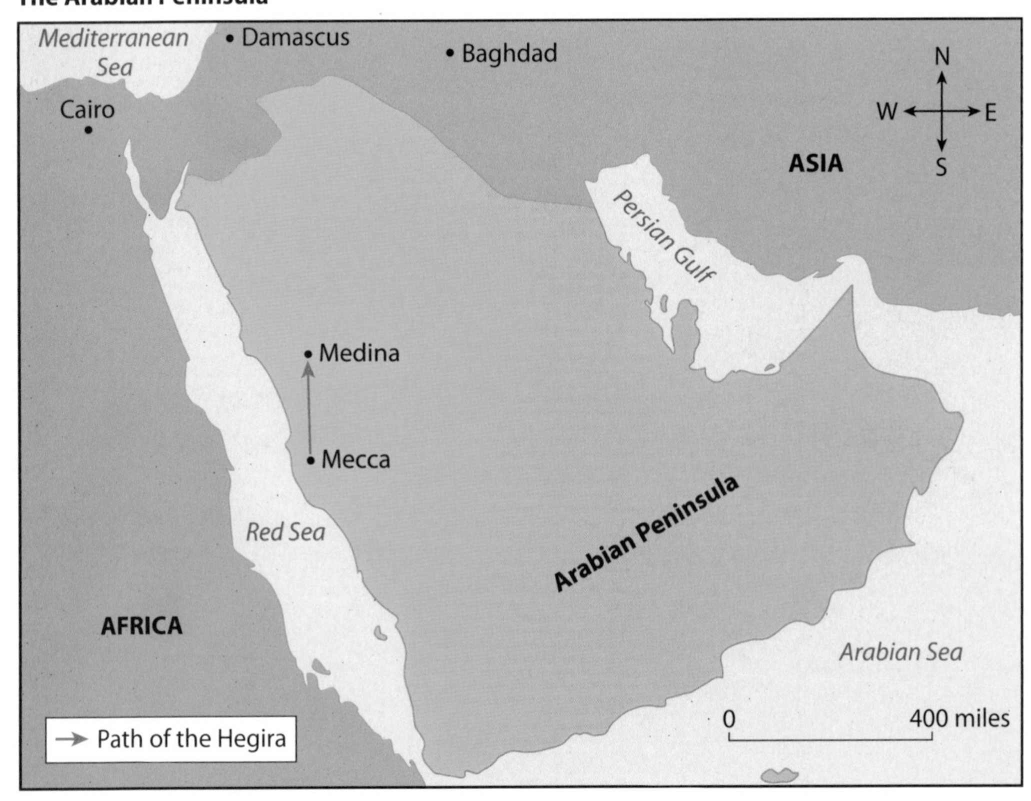

The map shows the journey from Mecca to Medina.

Some Meccans were so upset by Muhammad's teaching that they planned to kill him. In September 622, when he learned of his enemies' plans, Muhammad and a trusted friend secretly left Mecca. They traveled on little-used routes to Medina. Many people in Medina welcomed Muhammad, including those who followed other religions, such as the Jewish people who followed Judaism.

The escape of Muhammad and his followers from Mecca to Medina is very important to Muslims. This event is called the *Hegira* (/hih*jye*ruh/). The Muslim calendar dates from the year in which the Hegira took place.

In the Hegira, Muhammad and his followers fled to the city of Medina.

Chapter 3
Islamic Expansion

From Medina to Mecca Again

> **The Big Question**
>
> Why was the flight to Medina the start of a new period in the history of Islam?

The Hegira, Muhammad's flight to Medina, marked the beginning of a new period in the history of Islam. Muhammad tried hard to **convert** the citizens of Medina to Islam. He concentrated on building a community among the people of Medina. He began to give Islam its own distinctive features.

> **Vocabulary**
>
> **convert,** v. to change from one belief or religion to another

Followers of Christianity and Judaism called people to prayer by using wooden clappers or rams' horns. Muhammad appointed a crier, or muezzin, to call Muslim believers to prayer.

The city of Medina, which welcomed Muhammad, is still considered holy by Muslims.

Jews fasted on the Day of Atonement, which came once a year. Muhammad's followers fasted between sunrise and sunset during the entire month of Ramadan, the ninth month of the Islamic calendar. Jews prayed toward Jerusalem, their holy city. Muslims also first prayed toward Jerusalem until Muhammad instructed them to pray toward the Kaaba in Mecca. Jews set aside Saturday as their holy day of the week. Christians chose Sunday. Muslims chose Friday.

Muhammad converted some of the people of Medina to Islam, though generally most Jewish people there resisted and continued to follow their own religion. Then conflicts appeared between the Jews of Medina and the followers of Muhammad. Eventually,

Upon returning to Mecca, Muhammad and his followers destroyed the statues of gods in the Kaaba and dedicated the shrine to Allah alone.

the Jewish people of Medina were either driven out, killed, or enslaved. Muhammad also spread Islam to other communities throughout the Arabian Peninsula. The merchants of Mecca, however, were not pleased. Meccans launched several attacks on Medina but were turned back. Finally, in 630, backed by a large force, Muhammad entered Mecca. Few Meccans fought against him. Muhammad destroyed the statues or idols of the many gods in the Kaaba. He restored the Kaaba into a holy place dedicated to Islam's God alone. Mecca was now the center of Islam.

Muhammad's Final Years

Muhammad lived two more years after his return to Mecca. During this time, Islam continued to spread throughout the Arabian Peninsula. Muslim warriors helped spread Islam by conquering neighboring communities. Muhammad taught that Muslims must spread God's law.

Thirty years passed between Muhammad's first vision and his death. Muslims believe Muhammad continued to receive **revelations** from Allah during this time. After his death the revelations were collected in a single book, the Koran. Muslims believe the Koran is the final word of God. As the final word, it does not contain any errors.

Vocabulary

revelation, n. something that is made known to humans by God

Some of his followers thought Muhammad would live forever, but in 632 he became ill. The man known as God's messenger died.

ونادى نوح ربه فقال رب إن ابني من أهلي وإن

وعدك الحق وأنت أحكم الحاكمين قال يا نوح إنه ليس من أهلك إنه
عمل غير صالح فلا تسئلن ما ليس لك به علم إني أعظك أن تكون من الجاهلين
قال رب إني أعوذ بك أن أسئلك ما ليس لي به علم وإلا تغفر لي وترحمني
أكن من الخاسرين قيل يا نوح اهبط بسلام منا وبركات عليك و
على أمم ممن معك وأمم سنمتعهم ثم يمسهم منا عذاب أليم تلك من أنباء الغيب
نوحيها إليك ما كنت تعلمها أنت ولا قومك من قبل هذا فاصبر إن العاقبة
للمتقين وإلى عاد أخاهم هودا قال يا قوم اعبدوا الله ما لكم

من إله غيره إن أنتم إلا مفترون يا قوم لا أسئلكم

عليه أجرا إن أجري إلا على الذي فطرني أفلا تعقلون ويا قوم استغفروا
ربكم ثم توبوا إليه يرسل السماء عليكم مدرارا ويزدكم قوة إلى قوتكم
ولا تتولوا مجرمين قالوا يا هود ما جئتنا ببينة وما نحن بتاركي آلهتنا
عن قولك وما نحن لك بمؤمنين إن نقول إلا اعتراك بعض آلهتنا بسوء
قال إني أشهد الله واشهدوا أني بريء مما تشركون من دونه فكيدوني
جميعا ثم لا تنظرون إني توكلت على الله ربي وربكم ما من دابة إلا هو آخذ
بناصيتها إن ربي على صراط مستقيم فإن تولوا فقد أبلغتكم ما

أرسلت به إليكم ويستخلف ربي قوما غيركم ولا

Handwritten Koran

Muhammad's First Successors

When Muhammad died, he appears to have left no instructions for choosing a successor. His followers had considered him the last of the prophets. The Muslims knew, however, that they needed strong leadership if they were going to survive. But Muhammad's death caused conflict over who was the rightful leader of the Islamic community. Muhammad's successors were called **caliphs** (/kay*lihfs/). Muhammad had a surviving daughter, but not a son. Two men stood ready to take over. They were Ali, Muhammad's cousin and his daughter's husband, and Abu Bakr, the father of one of Muhammad's wives and one of Muhammad's closest friends. The important elders of Medina chose Abu Bakr. But Abu Bakr, the first caliph, lived for only two more years. The second Caliph was Umar, another close companion of Muhammad's. Once again, Ali was overlooked. Within twenty-four years of Muhammad's death, there was a civil war that created the two branches of Islam—the Shiite, who are the followers of Ali, and the Sunni.

Vocabulary

caliph, n. a successor of Muhammad; the leader of Islam

Despite such conflict, Islam spread far and wide. The first four caliphs conquered land throughout Syria, Egypt, North Africa, and Persia.

Muslim warriors depended on military strategy and good fortune. In one important battle for the city of Damascus in Syria, for example, a much larger army outnumbered the Muslim warriors.

The Muslims camped with the desert at their backs, waiting for the enemy forces to follow them. When the two armies met in the

Damascus became the capital of an Islamic empire.

battle on a hot summer day, a strong wind blew in from behind the Muslim troops, swirling dust and sand and blinding the enemy forces. The Muslim warriors were able to win an important victory. The great ancient Syrian city of Damascus was theirs.

Within one hundred years after the death of the Prophet Muhammad, Muslim rule had spread from the Arabian Peninsula to the borders of India and China in the east. It spread through North Africa and into Spain in the west. Muslim armies also advanced as far as Constantinople, the capital of the Byzantine Empire, conquering it in 1453.

Although Muslim caliphs ruled this vast territory, most conquered people did not immediately convert to Islam.

This took hundreds of years. However, over time most conquered people did convert.

The caliphs worked to organize and govern their growing empire. They used their powerful armed forces to control that empire. They collected taxes. They made Arabic the official language of the government.

The caliphs also created a special place for other believers who worshipped one God. Jews and Christians were known as "People of the Book." Muslims believed that Jews and Christians worshipped the same God as Muslims. As "People of the Book," Jews and Christians had more rights and privileges than other non-Muslims, although they did pay a tax. This tax, according to Islamic law, provided them with protection and released them from having to serve in the army.

The Spread of Islam

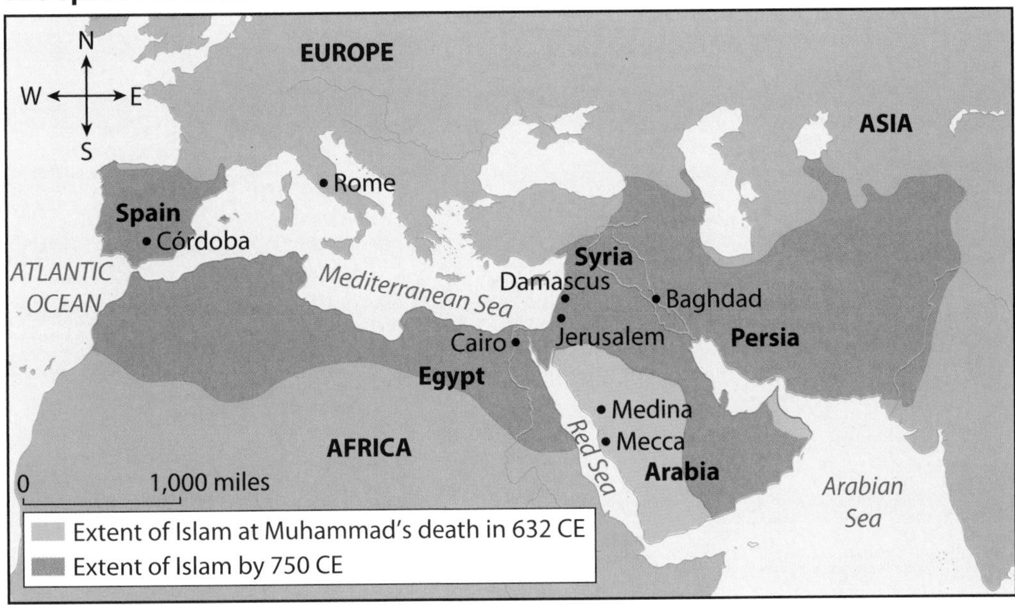

This map shows how far Islam spread from the time of Muhammad's death in 632 to 750 CE.

Chapter 4
Islamic Culture

Islamic Civilization Thrives For the first hundred years or so, Islam spread mostly through conquest. Then, when new rulers took control of the empire, they moved the center of government from Damascus to Baghdad, in what is now Iraq. Baghdad became the center of a great empire. The new rulers did not conquer much new land. Instead, they strengthened their empire though trade, agriculture, and learning.

The Big Question

How did the Islamic Empire contribute to the development of Western knowledge and culture?

Traders crossed the empire exchanging goods from India, Arabia, North Africa, and the Ottoman Empire. Traders also exchanged ideas, customs, and practices. The Islamic Empire had conquered many ancient centers of learning, such as Alexandria in Egypt. Traders and government officials brought the writings they found to Baghdad and other great Islamic cities.

As the capital of an Islamic empire, Baghdad became a center of trade and learning.

Muslim scholars translated the works of Greek philosophers such as Plato, Aristotle, Galen, and many other great scholars into Arabic. They saved many original works of Greek and Roman thinkers. These works opened up new levels of understanding for Muslim thinkers. Centuries later, the same would happen for Europeans, who rediscovered the ancient works, thanks to the work of Muslim **scribes**.

Vocabulary

scribe, n. a person whose job is copying written information

navigation, n. the act of planning and directing the movement of a ship, plane, or other vehicle

Other manuscripts were translated into Arabic from their original languages. Indian writings introduced the numerals 0 through 9. Indian mathematicians also introduced the place-value system.

Muslim scholars greatly improved the accuracy of the astrolabe, which was used for navigation and astronomy.

These numerals have been used since that time throughout the world. The mathematics in your textbooks today is based on these numerals and this place-value system. In the 800s, Muslims called these numerals "Hindi numbers," after the language of northern India. However, since their translation into Arabic, they have been called "Arabic numbers."

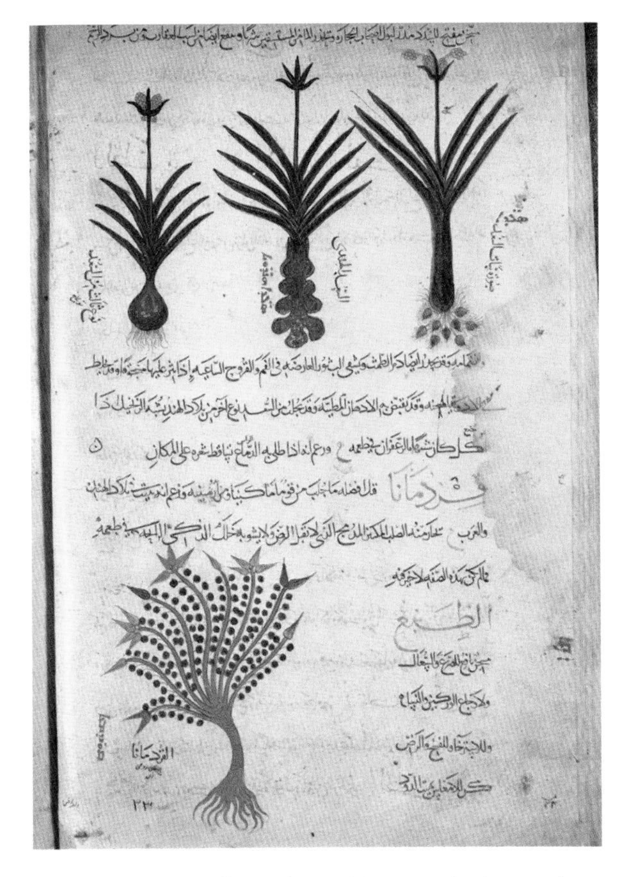

This manuscript from the 1100s reveals the study of the parts of plants.

Learning and Discovery

Muslim scholars didn't just translate ancient works. They made great advances in many fields, including philosophy, astronomy, medicine, and mathematics.

One mathematician, Muhammad al-Khwarizmi, created an entirely new form of mathematics—**algebra**. He built on the work of Greek mathematicians to create new ways of working with numbers.

> **Vocabulary**
>
> **algebra,** n. a type of advanced mathematics

In medicine, Muslim doctors were far ahead of those in western Europe. Muslim doctors were the first to describe measles and smallpox accurately. They were the first to discover how some diseases spread. One doctor and philosopher, Ibn Sina, was especially influential.

Ibn Sina was born in 980 CE. He was a wonder child. It is said that he memorized the Koran by the time he was ten and learned medicine and philosophy by the time he was a teenager. The Koran has 114 chapters and more than 6,000 verses! As an adult he wrote a detailed medical encyclopedia, the *Canon of Medicine*, and a review of all the philosophical sciences of his day. The encyclopedia was used to teach doctors throughout the Muslim world. Later, it was translated and used in Europe for hundreds of years.

Muslim doctors were the first to understand measles and smallpox.

Ibn Sina described various diseases and their treatments with great accuracy. He also wrote a philosophical text titled *The Healing*. His interests didn't stop there, however. He also wrote books on astronomy and mathematics.

Eventually, the works of Ibn Sina and other Islamic scholars were shared with Europe. Muslims conquered southern Spain in the late 700s. The Spanish city of Córdoba became a center of Muslim art and learning. Córdoba boasted three thousand mosques, seven hundred libraries, and several universities. Muslim scholars in Spain also translated works from Arabic and Hebrew and Latin. By 1150, European doctors were reading translations of Ibn Sina's medical encyclopedia and philosophical works. By 1200, Europeans had been introduced to algebra.

La Mezquita—the Great Mosque of Córdoba—was built in 784. Later, it was turned into a Catholic cathedral.

Architecture and Art

During this time art and architecture also thrived. Some of the most beautiful buildings in the world were designed by Muslim architects. The Great Mosque of Samarra, in Iraq, is one of these buildings.

Muslim artists created complex patterns and designs in bright colors. They applied these patterns to all types of surfaces: pottery, tile, glass, wood, plaster, **stucco**, and even brick. Islamic artists developed **calligraphy**, the art of elegant writing. Muslims often used calligraphy to write words from the Koran. Thus, they turned the words into works of art.

Vocabulary

stucco, n. a type of rough plaster; a material used to make walls

calligraphy, n. artistic handwriting

Muslim poets wrote poems of great beauty. Other Muslim writers told stories that are still read today. One of the greatest story

This doorway is decorated with Islamic patterns and calligraphy.

collections in Muslim literature is *A Thousand and One Nights*, also known as *The Arabian Nights*.

While Muslim scholars, poets, and architects created great treasures, Islam continued to spread, by way of preaching, by trade, and by warfare. People in East Africa, West Africa, South Asia, and Southeast Asia converted to Islam.

During this time a new group of Muslims, the Seljuk (/sel*jook/) Turks, took control of much of the Islamic Empire. They did not stop there. By 1100, the Seljuk Turks had seized more than half of the old Byzantine Empire.

Chapter 5
The Crusades

A Call for Help Near the end of the 1000s, the Byzantine emperor, Alexius I, asked Pope Urban II for help. Seljuk Turks were conquering parts of the Byzantine Empire. The emperor wanted help turning them back.

The Big Question

What events caused the First Crusade?

Urban II was the religious leader of Christians in western Europe. The Byzantines were members of the Eastern Orthodox Christian Church. The emperor did not ask for help regaining his empire. Instead, he cleverly stressed the need for *all* Christians, whether they were from the west or the east, to unite against Muslims. Muslims also had control of Jerusalem and Palestine, known as the Holy Land. The emperor asked for help to conquer the Holy Land.

The Holy Land (present-day Israel and Palestine) was the place in the Middle East where Jesus had once lived. It had been under Muslim control for nearly four hundred years. During most of that time, many Christian pilgrims traveled to the Holy Land to pray and to visit the places sacred to Christianity. But Turkish conquests had made traveling to the Holy Land difficult.

The pope called on European Christians to reconquer the Holy Lands in the Middle East.

Many European knights answered the pope's call to free the Holy Land from Muslim control.

Pope Urban II responded as the Byzantine emperor had hoped. He delivered a stirring speech in 1095, urging all Christians to free the Holy Land. The Christians, assembled in a field, listened to Urban's powerful call for war against the Muslims. Many were eager to take up this **cause**. Within a month, **crusaders** from western Europe were marching off to war.

War

A series of bloody wars followed when Christians from Europe set off to fight Muslims for control of the Holy Land. In Europe, these wars were called the Crusades. The word "crusade" comes from the Latin word *crux* meaning "cross."

Among Muslims, these wars were called "the Frankish invasions." The Arabic word for all Europeans in general was "Franks." Muslims saw the Christian armies as invaders of their land.

Vocabulary

cause, n. something that a group of people believe in or fight for

crusader, n. someone who participated in religious wars during the Middle Ages in which Christians from Europe attempted to take back the Holy Land and other territories from Muslims in the Middle East

heretic, n. a person who does not accept or follow the ideas of a particular religion

These clashes, from 1095 to 1272, were a sad chapter in history. Western Christians were eager to expel or convert nonbelievers. They attacked not only Muslims, but also Jews and eastern Christians, whom they also considered **heretics**. Muslims defended the lands they had conquered more than four hundred years before. Muslims generally respected Christians as fellow believers in one God and considered them as "People of the Book." However, they did not want western Christians conquering their land. The result was nearly two hundred years of gruesome warfare.

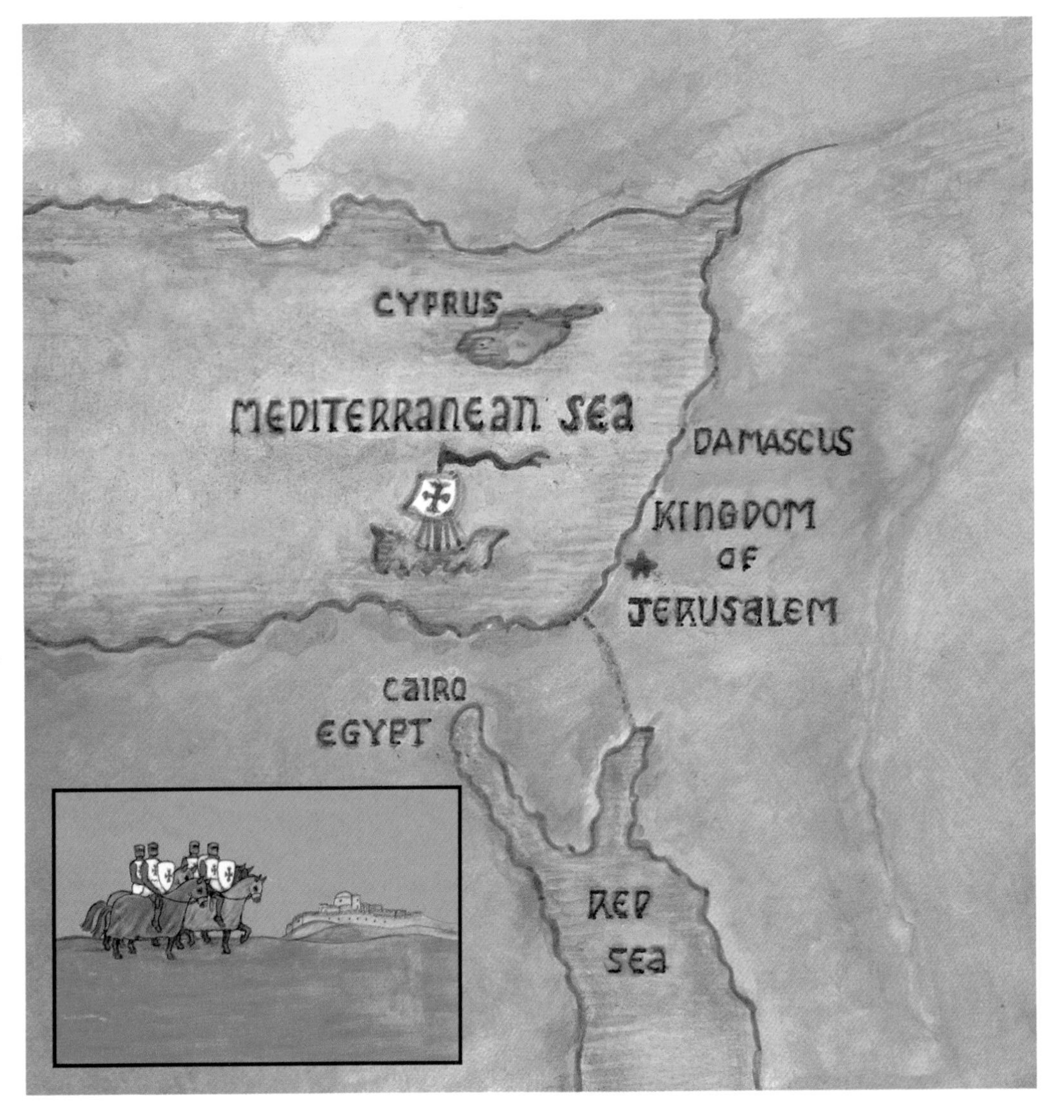

During the Crusades, European crusaders fought Muslim armies for control of Palestine.

The Europeans sent eight Crusades from Europe. Only the First Crusade brought the Europeans military success. They gained some territory in Palestine, including Jerusalem. Over time, however, the Muslims gained back all the territory they had lost.

Richard and Saladin

The Third Crusade (1189–1192) is perhaps the most famous because the leaders of both sides were heroes to their followers. The crusaders were led by King Richard I of England, known as Richard the Lionhearted. The Muslims were led by Saladin, the sultan, or ruler, of Egypt and Syria.

Saladin became sultan of Egypt and Syria in 1169. He was a courageous and skillful leader. He managed to unite Muslims from Egypt, Syria, Palestine, and Iraq. Saladin was committed to reconquering the land lost to the crusaders and bringing them back into the Islamic fold. He founded Islamic schools and universities. He also strengthened the army. After a truce with the crusaders failed in 1187, Saladin began to reconquer areas of the Holy Land. Soon, he had recaptured Jerusalem. Saladin did not

Saladin united Muslims to reclaim the Holy Land from European crusaders.

allow his soldiers to kill the inhabitants of Jerusalem. He left the holy city's shrines and churches unharmed.

> **Vocabulary**
>
> **infidel,** n. someone who does not believe in a certain religion or rejects its teachings

The pope called for a new Crusade after the Muslim capture of Jerusalem. King Richard responded to the call.

Loved by his subjects, Richard was everything a knight in the Middle Ages was supposed to be. He was brave in warfare, a fearless leader whom men were willing to follow into battle. It is said that he put everything he owned up for sale to raise money for the Third Crusade.

Both Richard and Saladin were men of courage and were willing to fight for their religions. They were both convinced that the other was an **infidel** and that the Holy Land should be theirs. But they admired each other's bravery and skill in battle.

England's King Richard I led Europeans in the Third Crusade.

The crusaders under Richard never did retake Jerusalem. However, the two sides came to an agreement. The European Christians would give up some of their land along the Mediterranean Sea. Saladin permitted Christians to make pilgrimages to the Holy Land, provided they came unarmed. Richard agreed to these terms and returned to England.

Some Effects of the Crusades

By the end of the last Crusade, the Muslims had reclaimed all the territories they had lost. Years of brutal warfare left Muslims and Christians suspicious and distrustful of each other.

Nevertheless, the Crusades allowed European nobles and Muslim leaders to learn from each other. In particular, western Europe benefited from Muslim scientific and cultural advances. By 1140, universities in western Europe taught the Arabic language. Western European scholars used Islamic scholarly texts. Arabic works, like those of Ibn Sina—known in the West by the Latin name Avicenna—were being translated into Latin. Trade was on the rise. Distrust remained, but it existed alongside a new curiosity.

The Ottoman Turks

By 1453 the Islamic Empire was dominated by another group of Turks: the Ottoman Turks. They had grown powerful enough to capture Constantinople. This city had been the center of the Byzantine Empire for more than 1,100 years. The Ottomans gathered a large fleet of ships and many warriors for an attack on Constantinople.

This painting shows the siege of Constantinople, which was finally conquered by the Ottoman Turks in 1453.

On May 29, 1453, the Ottomans captured this prize of the Byzantine Empire. They changed its name to Istanbul, from a Greek word meaning "into the city." Istanbul would be a major center of Islam for centuries to come.

The Ottomans did not stop at Constantinople. Over the next seventy-five years, they pushed into southeastern Europe. They were halted first in 1529 at Vienna, in present-day Austria. In 1571 the navies of western Europe dealt the Ottomans a decisive defeat. The Ottomans stopped expanding into Europe.

For hundreds of years, Islamic armies had successfully defended themselves and conquered new lands. Islamic cultural accomplishments had continued to grow, too. Islam influenced people around the world. We still benefit from its scientific and mathematical advances. We still marvel at the riches of its art.

Glossary

A

algebra, n. a type of advanced mathematics (29)

C

caliph, n. a successor of Muhammad; the leader of Islam (23)

calligraphy, n. artistic handwriting (32)

cause, n. something that a group of people believe in or fight for (37)

clan, n. a group of families claiming a common ancestor (14)

convert, v. to change from one belief or religion to another (18)

crusader, n. someone who participated in religious wars during the Middle Ages in which Christians from Europe attempted to take back the Holy Land and other territories from Muslims in the Middle East (37)

H

heretic, n. a person who does not accept or follow the ideas of a particular religion (37)

I

idol, n. an object, such as a statue or carving, that represents a god and is worshipped (8)

infidel, n. someone who does not believe in a certain religion or rejects its teachings (40)

M

meditate, v. to think quietly or carefully about something (15)

minaret, n. a high tower on a mosque, from which Muslims may be called to prayer (2)

mosque, n. a place of worship for Muslims (4)

muezzin, n. a religious official who calls Muslims to prayer (2)

N

navigation, n. the act of planning and directing the movement of a ship, plane, or other vehicle (28)

P

pilgrimage (hajj in Arabic), n. a journey undertaken for a religious purpose (4)

prophet, n. someone chosen by God to bring a message to people (4)

R

Ramadan, n. a holy month in the Islamic calendar when Muslims fast from sunrise to sunset (10)

revelation, n. something that is made known to humans by God (21)

S

sacred, adj. related to religion; holy (14)

scribe, n. a person whose job is copying written information (28)

shrine, n. a place considered holy because it is associated with a religious person or saint (8)

stucco, n. a type of rough plaster; a material used to make walls (32)

V

verse, n. a part of a poem, song, or religious text, such as the Bible, or rhymed prose, such as the Koran (6)

vision, n. an image in one's mind or imagination that others cannot see (6)

Early and Medieval African Kingdoms

Table of Contents

Reader

Core Knowledge History and Geography™

Chapter 1
The Geographic Setting

A Large Continent Africa is the second largest continent in the world after Asia. Africa is so large that you could fit Europe, the United States, China, and India inside of it. Africa stretches about 5,000 miles from its northern edge to its southern tip. It is about 4,600 miles at its widest east-west point. It is a land of deserts, rainforests, rivers, and grassy plains.

> **The Big Question**
>
> How might the geography of Africa have influenced the development of early African kingdoms and empires?

This map of North Africa was created by a Greek cartographer in 1522.

Seas and Oceans

Africa is surrounded by water. The Mediterranean Sea borders Africa on the north. It provides the continent with an important water route to Europe and western Asia. The ancient Greeks, Romans, and North Africans used the Mediterranean Sea for trade. In the Middle Ages, Muslims from North Africa traded with people in Europe and western Asia.

The stormy Atlantic Ocean borders Africa on the west. It kept Europeans away from western Africa for centuries. In the late 1400s, Europeans adapted Arab ships and technology to be able to sail the Atlantic. European explorers began to explore western and southern Africa.

The Indian Ocean borders Africa on the east. It is the third largest ocean in the world. It stretches about 4,500 miles from east to west from eastern Africa to Australia. It is about 6,000 miles north to south from India to Antarctica. The Indian Ocean linked people in Africa and Asia for centuries. Traders sailed between Africa, the Arabian Peninsula, and India. In the 1400s, Chinese fleets even reached the east African coast.

Madagascar is the world's fourth largest island. It lies in the Indian Ocean about 200 miles east of the African continent. The island is almost as big as Arizona and New Mexico combined. Africans and visitors from Asia explored the island thousands of years ago.

The Indian and Atlantic Oceans meet at the southern tip of Africa. It is a dangerous place for ships. The west coast of the southern

Physical Geography of Africa

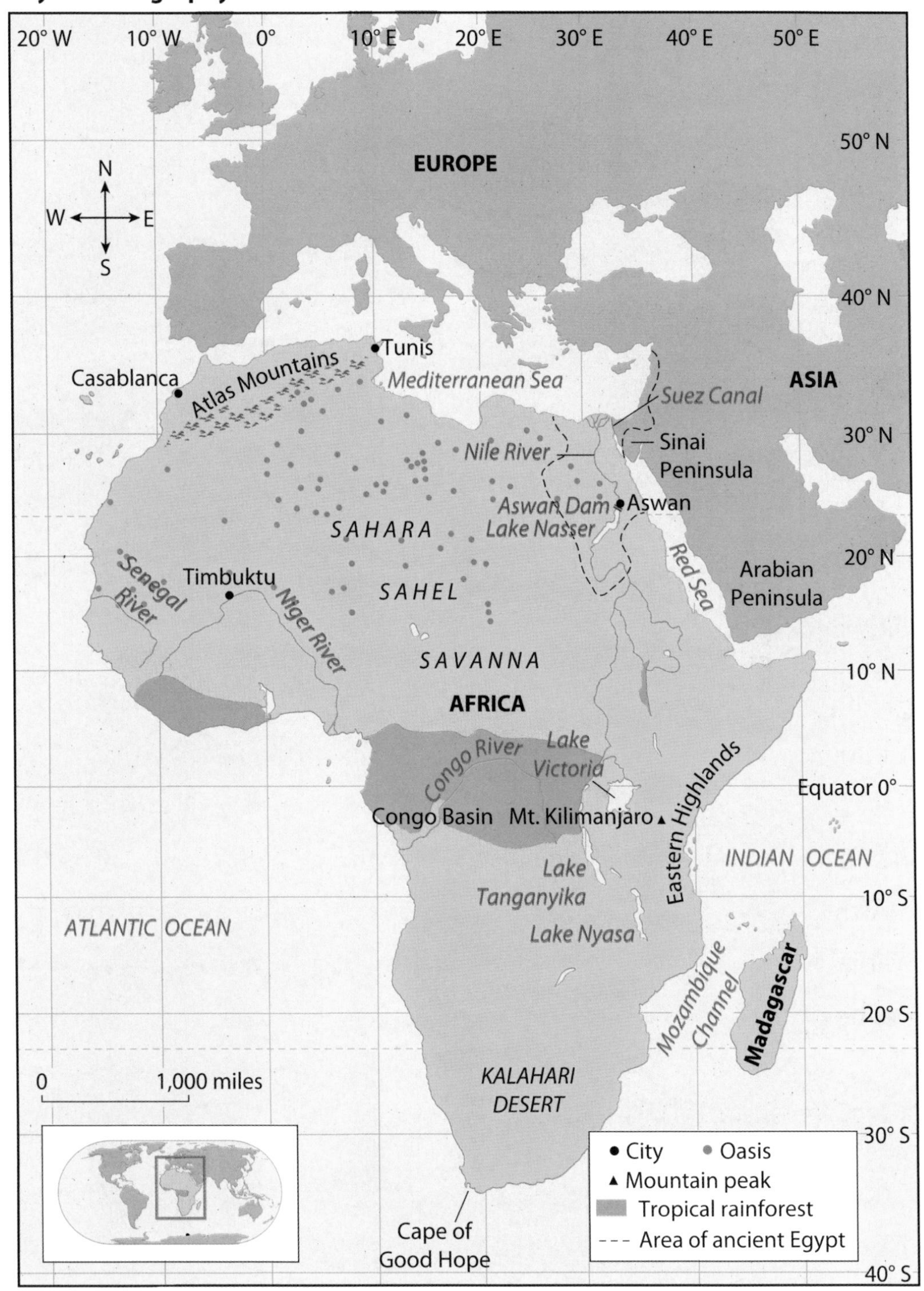

Africa, the world's second largest continent, is a land of diverse geographic features, including deserts, capes, and mountains.

part of Africa experiences many storms. Originally, Europeans called it the **Cape** of Storms. Later its name was changed to the Cape of Good Hope to make it sound more peaceful.

> **Vocabulary**
>
> **cape,** n. a point of land extending into water

The Red Sea lies off the northeastern coast of Africa. It separates the continent from Asia. The Red Sea extends northwest for about 1,200 miles from the southern edge of the Arabian Peninsula to the Sinai Peninsula in Egypt. For centuries, the Red Sea served as a major trade route between East Africa and Asia. Today, the Suez Canal links the Red and Mediterranean seas.

The Northwest Coast and Atlas Mountains

Africa has many different physical features and climates. We are going to work our way south from Africa's northern coast on the Mediterranean Sea to southern Africa. A narrow strip of land lies along northwestern Africa. It is mostly flat and has warm, rainy winters and hot, dry summers. This land lies between the Mediterranean Sea and the Atlas Mountains 200 miles to the south. It stretches east about 1,200 miles from the present-day city of Casablanca to the present-day city of Tunis. That's more than one third the width of the United States!

The Atlas Mountains form a barrier between northwest Africa and a large desert called the Sahara. There are no barriers between the Sahara and the Mediterranean in northeast Africa. The desert stretches right to the sea.

The Sahara

The Sahara is the largest desert on Earth. It is larger than the United States! It stretches south from the Atlas Mountains to the Sahel region of Africa. It extends east from the Atlantic Ocean to the Red Sea.

The Sahara experiences large changes in temperature. During the day, the temperature can reach 120°F. At night, the temperature can drop to 32°F. It rarely rains in the Sahara. However, when it does, the rain can be so heavy that it causes flash floods.

Some people imagine the Sahara as bands of golden sand. In fact, only about 20 percent of the Sahara is sand. The rest is rock and gravel. Some parts of the Sahara look like a rolling sea of sand. Other parts are hard, flat plains.

Parts of the Sahara look like a sea of sand.

The Sahara is dotted with **oases**. The water at these oases allows people to grow fig, olive, and date trees. They also grow other fruits and vegetables. Even today, travelers across the Sahara stop at oases to refill their water containers and get food. In the eastern Sahara, people use the Nile River for transportation and water.

Vocabulary

oasis, n. an area in the desert where there are water and plants

Although life in the Sahara can be harsh, nearly 2.5 million people live there today. Most of these people live in oases or near the Nile River. The desert is also home to many animals, including gazelles, scorpions, lizards, antelope, jackals, foxes, and hyenas.

Below the western Sahara is a strip of land called the Sahel. The Sahel separates the western Sahara from the more fertile lands to the south. The word *Sahel* means shore. It is like the shoreline between the "sea of sand" of the Sahara and the grasslands of the savanna.

The Sahel

The Sahel is a semi-dry rolling plain that stretches eastward across Africa from the Atlantic Ocean to the Indian Ocean. The region is an area of gradual change between the desert to the north and the savanna regions to the south.

Most of the Sahel receives ten to twenty inches of rain each year. Most rain tends to fall during the rainy season of June, July, and August. Various grasses and other types of plants that can survive with very little rain grow in the Sahel. The land is used mainly for grazing animals such as goats, sheep, and cattle. Some crops, such as peanuts, are raised there. To the south of the Sahel lies a large grassland called the savanna.

The Savanna

The savanna is a large region of tall grasses. It is dotted by trees and herds of animals. It reaches from the Atlantic Ocean in the west to the highlands of the present-day country of Ethiopia in the east.

In the drier parts of the savanna, broad rocky plains are crossed by deep **ravines**. Farther south, the region becomes wetter, with rolling hilly grasslands good for grazing herds of animals. Many **nomadic**

Vocabulary

ravine, n. a small, deep, narrow valley

nomadic, adj. moving around, often in search of food; not settled in one place

Animals, such as these giraffes, graze on the grasses of the savanna.

peoples raise their goats, sheep, and cattle on the savanna.

Vocabulary

sorghum, n. a type of grain fed to animals; also used for making a type of porridge for people to eat

The savanna has two seasons—wet and dry. During half the year, it rains, and rains, and rains. During the other half of the year, the air is dry and hot. This is called the "dry season."

There is enough rain to grow many crops on the savanna. These include grains such as corn, **sorghum**, and millet. Farmers also produce beans, peas, squash, melons, and okra. In areas with more rainfall, farmers grow rice, oranges, lemons, limes, and yams. Farmers clear their fields by burning the plants and then using the ashes as fertilizer.

The Rainforest

As you travel south of the savanna, temperatures remain warm but rainfall increases. Warm temperatures and heavy rainfall create tropical rainforests throughout central Africa. Africa's rainforests are covered with dense vegetation. They are similar to the rainforests of Brazil, Indonesia, and other parts of the world.

There aren't any "seasons" in tropical rainforests. The climate is the same all year. The temperature usually stays between 75 and 80°F. This part of Africa usually gets between 80 and 400 inches of rain a year. Because of this climate, the rainforest is home to thousands of different types of plants.

Southern Africa

South and east of its rainforests, Africa has a variety of climates and land features. Much of the land is rolling savannas. Other areas have mountains. The southwestern tip of Africa has a climate similar to that of northwest Africa. Southern Africa is also home to Africa's second major desert.

The Kalahari Desert is located in the present-day countries of Namibia, Botswana, and South Africa. It is covered with red soil and dry grasses. It is difficult to grow anything in the Kalahari because there is so little water. Still, wild animals such as meerkats, wildebeests, zebras, giraffes, and elephants live there. Some Khoikhoi and San peoples still survive in the Kalahari Desert by hunting, gathering, and herding. Others have been forced to move to villages.

Meerkats stand on the red sands of the Kalahari Desert.

Most of the land east of Africa's rainforests is savanna. However, the highest mountain in Africa is also found here. This mountain, Mount Kilimanjaro, is located in the country of Tanzania. Mountains are also found along Africa's southern coast.

African Rivers

Some of the world's greatest rivers slice through the African continent. The Niger and Senegal rivers flow through the savanna of West Africa. Some of the great **kingdoms** and **empires** of medieval Africa developed along these rivers. Among these were Ghana, Mali, and Songhai. You will learn more about them later.

> **Vocabulary**
>
> **kingdom,** n. a country ruled by a king or queen
>
> **empire,** n. a group of countries controlled by a single authority

The powerful Congo River flows through the hot rainforest region of Africa. The Congo is the second-longest river in Africa. It is about 2,720 miles long and flows from central Africa to the Atlantic Ocean.

Africa's most famous river is the Nile River. The Nile is the longest river in the world. The Nile starts at Lake Victoria in east-central Africa. It flows north to the Mediterranean Sea, for a total of more than 4,130 miles.

In ancient times, the Nile flooded its banks once a year. The flood water deposited rich, black soil nearby. Egyptian farmers planted their crops in this soil. They were able to grow more food than they needed. Grain raised along the Nile was sent to many places, including Rome. Since the 1970s, the huge Aswan High Dam in

Egypt controls the flooding of the Nile. A large lake, called Lake Nasser, has formed behind the dam. The waters from this lake are used to make electricity and to water farmlands.

The Egyptian Civilization

The geography of Africa played a big role in the development of early and medieval kingdoms and empires. The oldest of these kingdoms was Egypt. Egyptian civilization stretches back more than five thousand years, to about 3100 BCE. The Nile River, which runs through Egypt, helped this ancient civilization succeed. A Greek historian once called Egypt "the gift of the Nile."

Farmers of ancient Egypt produced a surplus of food. This allowed some Egyptians to do other things. They became the craftsmen, soldiers, officials, and other specialized workers who helped make civilization grow and prosper. The Nile River also played an important role in the development of the ancient kingdoms of Kush and Aksum. You will read about these kingdoms in the next chapter.

The Nile River is the longest river in the world. Today, just as thousands of years ago, it is used for transportation and to water fields.

Chapter 2
The Kingdoms of Kush and Aksum

Egypt's Rivals In addition to the great Egyptian civilization, other African civilizations thrived in ancient times. Two of these were Kush and Aksum.

> **The Big Question**
>
> How did trade contribute to the rise of the Kush and Aksum kingdoms?

Kush was the ancient Egyptian name for the African land of Nubia. It is located in eastern Africa, south of Egypt. Nubia was the home of an advanced civilization. Historians believe that the Kingdom of Kush began in about 2000 BCE. The Kushites were good farmers, metalworkers, and traders. Because of trade, they had contact with areas throughout eastern Africa.

> **Vocabulary**
>
> **natural resource,** n. something from nature that is useful to humans
>
> **goods,** n. items that people want to buy

Other than the Nile River, Egypt has few **natural resources** of its own. The Nile provided the water to help Egyptians grow food. For centuries, Egyptians traded the food they raised with the Kushites for other **goods**. The Kushites mined minerals and produced iron. They also traded with people from

Ancient Egyptians traded their extra grain with the Kushites for gold and other goods.

central Africa. Central Africans sold **ebony wood**, ivory, **incense**, and animal skins. Egyptians wore beautiful gold jewelry made by the Kushites. They decorated their homes with ivory and metalwork purchased in the marketplaces of Kush.

Vocabulary

ebony wood, n. a dark, hard wood that comes from tropical trees

incense, n. something that has a pleasant smell when it is burned

Kush Declines, Egypt Expands

In 1500 BCE, the Egyptians were the strongest kingdom in the area as Kush foreign trade and influence declined. They began establishing an empire by conquering the land around them. Egyptian armies conquered lands along the Mediterranean coast to the north and east. They also conquered lands along the Nile, to the south. This included the area of Kush.

Over the next five centuries, 1500 BCE – 1000 BCE, the Kush people seemed to become Egyptian. They wore Egyptian-style clothing and worshipped Egyptian gods. Yet underneath their borrowed robes, the Kush people kept their culture and identity. They adapted pieces of Egyptian culture to their own culture.

In about 730 BCE Egypt grew weak. The Kushites struck at the Egyptians with all their might and defeated them. For a few decades, Kushite rulers became the pharaohs of Egypt. This was a great period in the history of Kush. But it lasted only 150 years. In 591 BCE, the Egyptians struck back, defeating Kush and capturing its capital.

The Kush people moved their capital farther south along the Nile to the city of Meroë (/muhr*oh*ee/). Meroë was surrounded by fine grazing land for herds of cattle, goats, and sheep. It was a major trading center. It was also one of Africa's first iron-producing centers. Kush shipped its ironwork across Africa. Incredible rumors of Kush's wealth spread far beyond Africa. The region was called the "Land of Gods."

Land of Wonders

The Greek historian Herodotus recorded some of the stories that had reached him about Meroë. Herodotus had heard about stone pyramids and a temple covered with sheets of gold shining like beacons in the bright African sun. Indeed, dozens of stone pyramids still stand outside Meroë. These pyramids are steeper than Egyptian pyramids and have flat tops. They were used as burial sites for the Kushite kings, just as the Egyptian pyramids were used as tombs for the pharaohs.

Unlike the pyramids of Egypt, some of Kush's pyramids had flat tops.

The gold bracelet was worn by a Kushite queen of Meroë.

Archaeologists have found jewelry and other valuable **artifacts** in these burial sites. These findings tell us that Meroë was once a wealthy place.

> **Vocabulary**
>
> **archaeologist,** n. an expert in the study of ancient people and the objects from their time period that remain
>
> **artifact,** n. an object used during a past period in history

A Bitter Fate

The Kush kingdom ended when it was attacked by its southern neighbor, Aksum, (also spelled Axum). Aksum was a kingdom located in present-day Ethiopia and Eritrea. As a result of war, Aksum destroyed the Kush kingdom. Early in the 300s CE, Aksum's great warrior-king Ezana conquered Kush.

The Kingdoms of Egypt, Kush, and Aksum

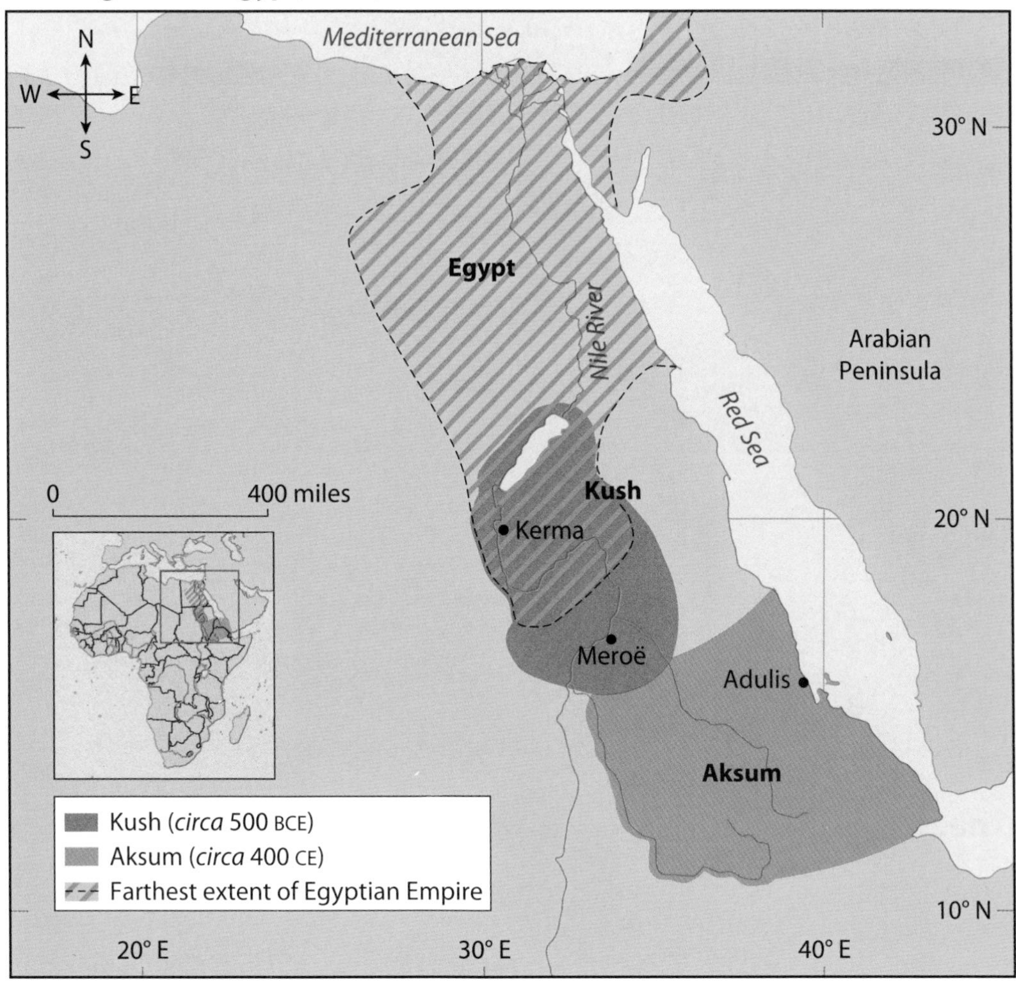

The three great kingdoms, Kush, Aksum, and Egypt, were all located in northeastern Africa.

Aksum

After Aksum defeated Kush, the trade routes through Kush were ignored. Instead, traders traveled to Aksum by sea. Trade flourished at Aksum's bustling port of Adulis on the Red Sea. Traders exchanged goods from eastern Africa as well as Egypt, India, and Rome. Over time, Aksum became the strongest power in eastern Africa. Travelers to Aksum commented on the wealth of the kings, their gold-embroidered clothes, and their chariots drawn by elephants.

Aksum prospered for several centuries. King Ezana had converted to Christianity, and Aksum became a Christian outpost in eastern Africa. Its kings built many churches and monasteries. They had the Bible translated into the local language, Ge'ez. Aksum also conquered neighboring lands, including part of the Arabian Peninsula.

The Christians of Aksum created religious images and symbols.

Over time, Aksum began to decline, especially as their major competitor, the Persians, pushed them out of Yemen across the Red Sea. At the same time, during the 700s CE, Muslims began to move from the Arabian Peninsula and into Africa. They took over many of the trade routes that had made Aksum a mighty kingdom. Eventually, the Muslims took over the seaport of Adulis. The Aksumite Christians converted to Islam or retreated into the mountains. Today many residents of the area are still Christian.

Chapter 3
Trans-Sahara Trade

> **The Big Question**
>
> How did trade help spread ideas?

Traders of Medieval Africa "I hope we're near the oasis," Yusef the trader sighed. Sweat dripped into his eyes. The sun stood at its highest point, and the air shimmered with heat. Yusef's throat was dry with thirst. His tongue was so dry that it felt like a slab of wood in his mouth.

Yusef felt like sitting down to rest, but he plodded on beside his camels. "It will be worth all this trouble when my salt fetches a great price at market," he whispered to himself. "Then I can buy more camels and become an important trader."

> **Vocabulary**
>
> **caravan,** n. a group of travelers journeying together, often across a desert

Like the other traders in this **caravan**, Yusef was transporting salt mined from the salt regions in the middle of the Sahara. The caravan was headed to a trading center in the Sahel, on the southern edge of the Sahara.

In the 700s CE, when Arabs of the eastern Mediterranean conquered North Africa and Spain, the trade routes were extended even farther. Camels were often called "ships of the desert" because they carried goods and people across vast deserts. Trade helped transport new ideas from the east to Spain and beyond.

At the mines, Yusef had watched the enslaved workers dig out 200-pound cakes of salt. They tied two cakes on each camel. "There is so much salt here that we build houses and **mosques** from it," the salt **quarry** owner had said. Yusef had actually seen a couple of these salt houses. They glittered in the sunlight. Now, Yusef's camels swayed under the 400-pound loads of salt they were hauling south.

> **Vocabulary**
>
> **mosque,** n. a place of worship for Muslims
>
> **quarry,** n. a place where stone or minerals are taken from the earth
>
> **splay,** v. to spread out

Ships of the Desert

Yusef's camels were smelly, and they often spat at their master. But Yusef was glad to have them. He knew that camels were made for the desert. Broad **splayed** feet let them walk over hot sand without sinking. A double row of eyelashes kept out stinging sand from windstorms. They stored fat in their humps. A camel could live off this fat when there was no food available. Camels could also go without water for days. Yusef was glad his precious cargo was carried on camels, not the horses used for the first desert caravans.

Yusef's last trip had gone smoothly, with nothing more than stinging bites from sand fleas. But Yusef knew that many traders ran into big problems on their journeys. Yusef had heard stories about traders who got caught in fierce sandstorms. Other traders got lost and had to kill their camels for food. Sometimes even this desperate measure was not enough. Yusef's own cousin had marched into the desert as part of a caravan. Neither he nor his fellow travelers were ever heard from again. As Yusef thought of his cousin, a shiver ran down his spine.

Camels have splayed feet.

Yusef tried to forget about his cousin and the dangers of the desert. Instead, he thought about the goods he and others would buy when they arrived at the markets of the Sahel. He ran over in his mind what could be bought with salt: gold, silks, ivory, leather, and even enslaved workers.

On past trips, the leather pouch Yusef carried had been loaded with **cowrie shells** from the Indian Ocean and glass beads from Venice, Italy. Yusef had traded these for sweet dates and chewy figs from the oases he passed on the trade route.

Yusef knew that the powerful kingdoms and empires in the vast Sahel also sold enslaved workers. Enslaved workers were often prisoners of war. They came from lands that had been conquered by one African power or another.

Vocabulary

cowrie shell, n. a type of shell found in the Indian and Pacific oceans that was used as money in some cultures

The Kingdom of Ghana and Empires of Mali and Songhai

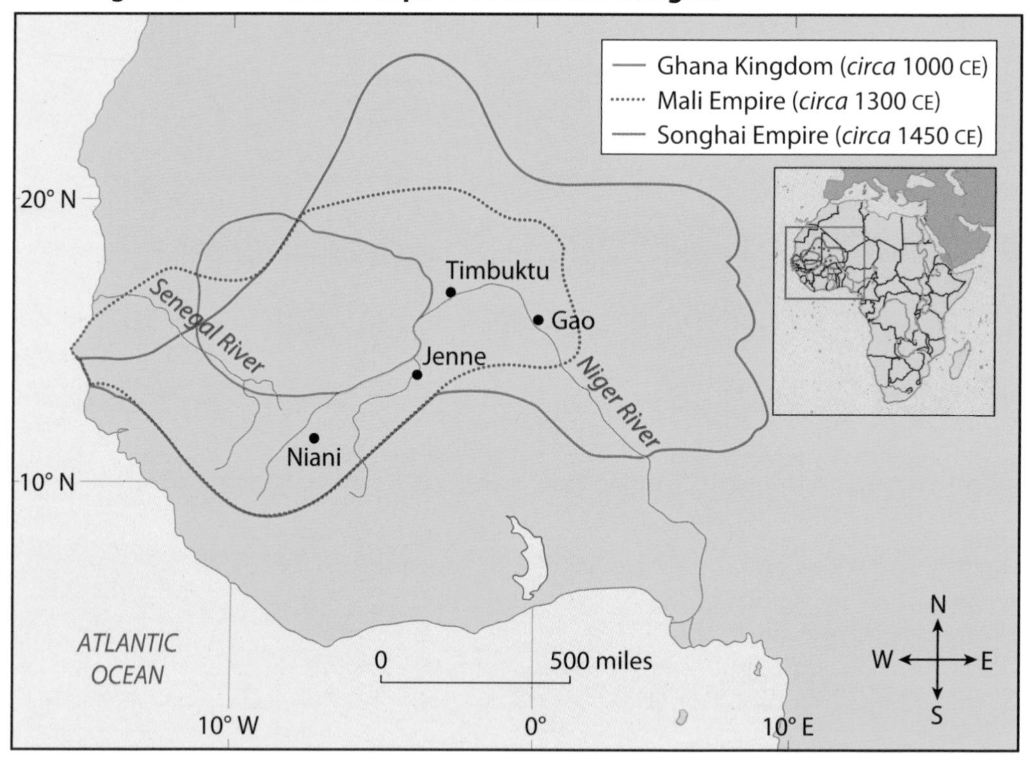

The kingdom of Ghana and the great empires of Mali and Songhai developed in the northwestern part of Africa.

West Africans also supplied the trans-Sahara traders with **kola nuts**, shea butter, and cloth. Traders like Yusef transported these items north and east. There they could trade them for more salt. And then the process would start all over again.

> **Vocabulary**
>
> **kola nut,** n. the fruit of the kola tree found in tropical regions of Africa

Traders Carry Precious Ideas

Caravans like Yusef's went back and forth across the desert for hundreds of years. Enslaved workers, gold, horses, salt, and other goods were not the only things they carried with them. The traders also carried things that couldn't be seen, felt, smelled, tasted, or heard. However, these things had far more impact than all the goods bought and sold.

What else did Yusef and his fellow traders carry? They carried ideas, art, culture, and religion.

Sometimes teachers, clerics, poets, musicians, and artists traveled with the traders. The teachers and poets on the caravan taught fellow travelers. The musicians sang their songs. The artists sold their work. Traders also brought their religion with them. Most of the traders were Muslim. They built mosques in the West African trading cities. They talked about Islam with people they met. By 1000 CE, many people in western Africa knew about the Islamic faith and culture.

Rulers in West African trading cities controlled the caravan trade. This control allowed them to develop large and powerful kingdoms and empires. Three great powers rose up in western Africa: Ghana, Mali, and Songhai.

Muslim traders built mosques in trading cities in West Africa.

Chapter 4
Ghana, Land of Gold

> **The Big Question**
>
> Why was salt almost as valuable as gold during this time?

A Kingdom Built on Gold King Tunka of Ghana sat on his throne in a huge, open building called a pavilion. Behind him stood servants holding shields and swords decorated with gold. To his right stood Ghana's noblemen and their sons. They wore beautiful robes and had gold threads braided into their hair.

The pavilion was in Ghana's royal capital of the twin city of Kumbi. Six miles away was the other city, Saleh. Officials of the kingdom stood near the king's throne. Even the animals wore gold. King Tunka's dogs wore gold and silver collars. Horses, covered with gold-embroidered cloth, pawed the ground outside the pavilion.

An early Arab explorer, al Bakri, talked to people who visited Kumbi. He claimed that the king of Ghana was the "wealthiest of all kings on the face of the earth." Muslim scholars called Ghana the "Land of Gold."

West African gold was the secret to Ghana's power.

How did Ghana become so rich?

Ancient Ghana was located between the upper Niger and Senegal rivers. Ghana's kings took advantage of their location. Salt mines lay to the north in the Sahara. Gold mines lay farther to the south. Trade routes between the mines ran right through Ghana. Another trade route ran east to the Nile River Valley. Ghana's capital, Kumbi, was at the center of these trade routes.

Ghana's location helped it become a great West African trading kingdom. The kingdom is said to have begun about 300 CE and lasted until the 1200s. It was largest in about 1000 CE. The kingdom of Ghana spread over an area almost as big as the state of Texas.

Vocabulary

tax, n. money that people are required to pay to support the workings of the government

Ghana's Great Kings

The kings helped the kingdom of Ghana grow by collecting **taxes** from traders passing through the area. Traders paid taxes on the goods they brought to sell and on the goods they purchased. These taxes went into the king's treasury and helped support his wealthy court. In return, the king protected the trade routes. The traders could travel safely throughout Ghana.

The people of Ghana created beautiful gold jewelry.

The king claimed all gold nuggets found in Ghana. He let traders keep the gold dust they brought from the gold mines. Gold mines lay south of Ghana along the Senegal River. The miners kept their exact location a secret. The gold was sometimes stuffed into hollow **quills** for safe travel across the Sahara.

Vocabulary

quill, n. the central part of a bird's feather, often used as a tool for writing

Salt, Vital for Life

You know that gold is valuable because it is rare and beautiful. But do you know why ancient Africans valued salt so highly? Africans prized salt for many important reasons. Salt kept meat and vegetables from spoiling in the hot weather. It made bland food tastier. Salt was also used as a medicine to treat many different illnesses. In addition, people in hot climates such as the Sahara needed—and still need—salt to replace the salt the body loses from sweating.

Although salt was plentiful in the northern deserts, it was rarer in western Africa. By the time a trader like Yusef had hauled his salt to western Africa, its value would have increased greatly. Salt was so valuable in this area that it was traded for an equal amount of gold.

Ghana Flourishes

Ghana became very rich and powerful by controlling the gold-salt trade. Ghana's kings used the profits made from this trade to build beautiful cities. Ghana's citizens admired the king's beautiful palace built of stone.

Iron ore was plentiful in Ghana and easy to mine. Ancient Ghanaians developed ways of working iron into strong tools and weapons. They used iron farming tools to increase the amount of food they could grow. They used iron weapons to win battles and expand their kingdom.

As traders passed through Ghana, they brought many new goods with them. Some traders paid their taxes in gold or salt. Others paid in copper, cloth, dried fruit, or other goods. As a result, the people of Ghana's cities had many fine things to purchase and enjoy.

Many traders from northern Africa and the Middle East moved to Ghana's cities to participate in the rich trade. Most of these traders were Muslims. The traders told the people they met about Islam. Some people of Ghana adopted this new religion. Most people continued to follow their traditional religious beliefs.

Traders from the Sahara carried slabs of salt to the markets of Ghana.

They worshipped one central god, many lesser gods, and spirits in nature. The religion of ancient Ghana also taught people to respect their ancestors.

Ghana's Downfall

Of course, neighbors envied a country as rich as Ghana. Enemies often attacked, hoping to get their hands on Ghana's gold.

Beginning in the late 900s, Ghana was attacked by various groups from North Africa. The Ghanaians fought off the first few attacks. However, in 1076, Kumbi was conquered. Muslim conquerors seized control. This was the beginning of Ghana's decline.

Ghana regained control of Kumbi in the late 1000s, but the kingdom never recovered its former power. As it became weaker, Ghana's gold production dropped. Ghana was further weakened when important trade networks slipped from its control.

In the early 1200s, Kumbi came under attack yet again. This time the attacker was a West African king named Sundiata Keita, whose people had previously served Ghana as a conquered state. In 1240 Sundiata Keita and his army captured Kumbi. They added the defeated kingdom of Ghana to the new empire of Mali.

Chapter 5
Mali and Sundiata Keita

The Big Question

Why might legendary stories have sprung up around Sundiata?

A Cruel King As Ghana's power decreased, many of the areas it had controlled became independent. One area was Mali. Mali eventually became the most powerful empire in West Africa. But during its early years, Mali was dominated by other powerful kingdoms.

Kirina was one of three towns that would form the foundation of Sundiata's empire of Mali. In this image, you can see grain stores used for keeping the grain dry.

One of Mali's early rivals was the Soso kingdom. The Soso lived in the coastal regions south of Ghana. Sumanguru (/su*man*gu*ru/), king of the Soso people, marched into Mali and conquered it. Cunning and cruel, Sumanguru taxed the people of Mali without mercy. He took their daughters and wives. To eliminate any rivals for his throne, Sumanguru decided to kill all of the former king's sons.

A Moment of Mercy

Sumanguru decided to spare the life of a young **Mandinka** prince named Sundiata (/sun*di*ah*ta/). Little Sundiata could not even stand up or walk. Even when he was seven, he crawled from place to place. Sumanguru decided that this child could not possibly be a threat to him.

Vocabulary

Mandinka, n. the group of people living in West Africa who ruled the Mali Empire

Sumanguru was wrong about that. Sundiata eventually grew up to be a great leader, known as "the hungering lion." Sundiata had a strong will. He refused to submit to his sickness. After months and months of trying, Sundiata forced himself to walk. Leaning on an iron cane, he hobbled around his village. Sundiata pushed himself further and harder. Years later, he was able to walk without a cane. Sundiata even became a great horseman and hunter.

The Mandinka people admired Sundiata and his bravery. They looked to Sundiata to rescue them from Sumanguru's hard rule. Sundiata's people counted on him to get rid of Sumanguru.

Sundiata versus Sumanguru

In 1230, the other leaders of Mali rallied around Sundiata. They proclaimed him the king of Mali. Sumanguru realized that Sundiata was a leader who could defeat him. But Sumanguru would not give up without a fight. He had a large, powerful army. His people believed that he had special powers that protected him from injuries during battle. Their belief in him made Sundiata's people strong, fearless warriors.

In 1235, Sumanguru's army met Sundiata's army in battle. During this battle Sundiata's Mali warriors crushed Sumanguru's army.

According to one Mandinka **legend**, Sumanguru disappeared when an arrow struck him. A giant tree sprung up where Sumanguru had stood. There are also legends that tell of Sundiata's bravery. Whichever legend you decide to believe, no one disagrees that Sundiata defeated Sumanguru. Sundiata had shown great bravery in battle. Even today, the Mandinka people celebrate Sundiata as a hero.

> **Vocabulary**
>
> **legend,** n. an old, well-known story that is usually more entertaining than truthful

Sundiata went on to conquer other lands. In 1240, he and his generals captured Kumbi, the old capital of Ghana. The empire of Mali became the most powerful empire in West Africa.

Mali's Power Grows

Like Ghana, Mali controlled West African trade. The leaders of Mali set up their capital in Niani. Mali had fair leaders. They created a strong government. They used trade and farming to help Mali become rich.

Sundiata proved to be as powerful a leader in peace as he had been in war. He created a strong central government that brought peace and order to the entire empire of Mali. This helped him regain control of the trade routes. Mali was self-sufficient in food production because villages and slave communities were purposefully organized for agricultural production. The leaders of Mali also increased trade in the cities along the Niger River. The new leaders of Mali took the proud title **mansa**, which means emperor.

Vocabulary

mansa, n. the title used by kings in the Mali Empire

A Muslim Empire

Islam had been a presence in West Africa since the kingdom of Ghana. However, most Mandinka did not convert to Islam until the end of the 1200s. Under a Muslim king, Islam became the most powerful religion in the Mali Empire. The Muslim holy book, the Koran, had become the basis of Mali culture. Mali had new laws, a tax system, and a dedication to education, all based on Islam.

The Great Mosque still stands in Timbuktu today.

Timbuktu, a Center of Learning

Many important cities developed and prospered in the Mali Empire. One of these was the capital city of Niani (/nee*ah*nee/). Others were the trading cities of Djenne, Gao, and Timbuktu.

Timbuktu is located at the bend of the Niger River. The people of the desert and the people of the river met at this spot to trade their goods. Over the years, Timbuktu grew from a group of tents into a great center for learning and trade. People throughout the Islamic world recognized its name.

Timbuktu had many mosques, libraries, and schools. The city also had a famous Muslim **university**. Muslim scholars throughout Africa traveled to Timbuktu to study at the university.

> **Vocabulary**
>
> **university,** n. a school where advanced learning is taught

A new ruler helped the world hear of Timbuktu and Mali. His name was Mansa Musa.

This painting from the 1800s shows Timbuktu hundreds of years ago.

Chapter 6
Mansa Musa and His Pilgrimage

The Big Question

What was so extraordinary about Mansa Musa's pilgrimage to Mecca?

A Glorious Reign Mansa Musa ruled Mali for twenty-five years, from 1307 to 1332. In that time, Mali's fame spread across the Sahara to the Middle East. It even spread across the Mediterranean Sea to Europe.

Mansa Musa extended Mali's borders far and wide. A trader passing through Mali in the 1330s described Mali as "square in shape." He said it took over four months to go from corner to corner of the large empire.

Mansa Musa also increased trade three times over. As many as twelve thousand camels passed through Mali every year. Mali's cities supplied water, food, and rest for the thirsty and weary travelers. Mansa Musa promoted education and the arts. He was especially interested in collecting books and in constructing new buildings. But above all, Mansa Musa was very religious.

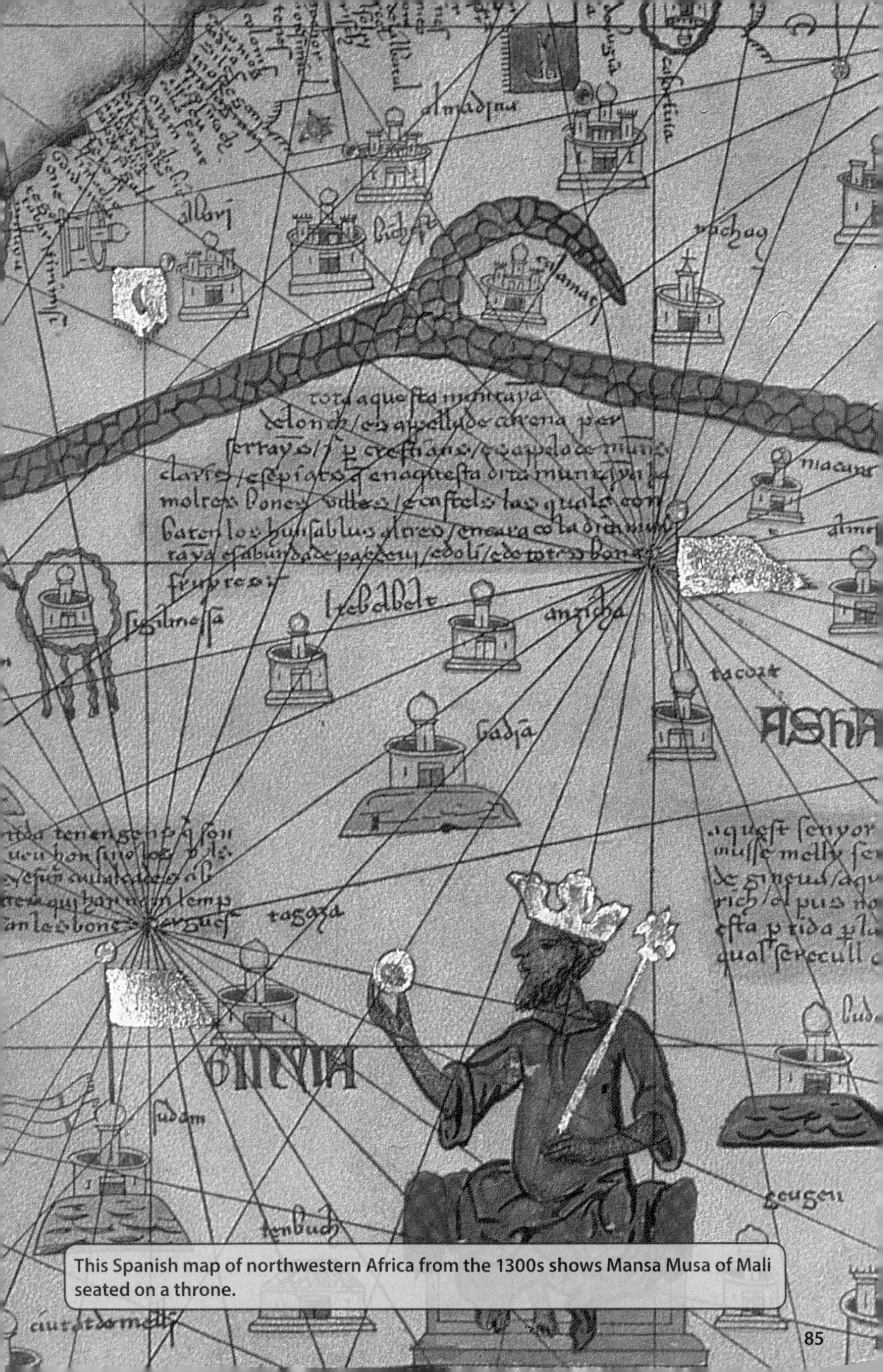

This Spanish map of northwestern Africa from the 1300s shows Mansa Musa of Mali seated on a throne.

A Golden Pilgrimage

In 1324, after converting to Islam, Mansa Musa decided to make a **pilgrimage** to Mecca, located in present-day Saudi Arabia. In Islam, Mecca is considered the holiest city in the Muslim world. Followers of Islam are required to travel to Mecca during their lifetime if they can afford to do so. Muslims call the pilgrimage to Mecca the *hajj*. Making the pilgrimage is one of the five pillars of Islam.

> **Vocabulary**
>
> **pilgrimage,** n. a journey undertaken for a religious purpose

The fact that Mansa Musa made a pilgrimage to Mecca wasn't unusual. Other West African rulers of Mali had already made pilgrimages there. It was how Mansa Musa made his pilgrimage that was so amazing.

Mansa Musa traveled with a huge caravan. Family, friends, teachers, and doctors came along. Mansa Musa also brought

A pilgrimage to Mecca is an important religious undertaking for Muslims.

along certain important chiefs. This was smart for two reasons. First, being part of Mansa Musa's pilgrimage brought honor to the chiefs. Second, getting the chiefs out of Mali reduced problems while Mansa Musa was away.

The caravan included thousands of people. It was very likely the biggest caravan ever to cross the Sahara. Mansa Musa also brought lots of gold. As a result, the caravan included as many as one hundred camels weighed down with sacks of gold.

> **Vocabulary**
>
> **lavish,** adj. rich or expensive

Sharing the Wealth

In 1324, Mansa Musa's extraordinary caravan entered Cairo, Egypt. Everyone in Cairo was impressed by Mansa Musa's wealth.

Mansa Musa's generosity was as impressive as his religious faith. Everywhere he stopped on his pilgrimage, Mansa Musa gave away gold. He gave **lavish** gifts of gold in the Muslim holy cities of Mecca and Medina. He gave gold to everyone who helped him on his journey, too. He gave away so much gold that the price of gold dropped in Cairo.

Mansa Musa supposedly gave away so much gold that the value of gold dropped.

On his return journey from Mecca back to Mali, Mansa Musa once more passed through Cairo—and gave away more gold.

"The Century of Musa"

Mansa Musa returned from his pilgrimage to Mecca in 1325.

Mansa Musa's son had done quite a good job ruling Mali during the time Mansa Musa had been on his pilgrimage. His son had even extended the empire to the east. He did this by conquering the city of Gao, the capital of the neighboring territory of Songhai. To make sure that Songhai would not revolt against Mali, Mansa Musa's son took two Songhai princes as **captives**.

> **Vocabulary**
>
> **captive,** n. a prisoner

Mansa Musa continued to support education and building in Mali. He persuaded a North African architect to return to Mali with him to build mosques in Mali's cities. He exchanged ambassadors with other Muslim countries such as Egypt and Morocco. He established religious schools to teach about Islam. However, he also allowed his people to choose which religion to follow. Some, including the people near the gold mines, continued to follow traditional religions.

Learning flourished in Mali during Mansa Musa's reign.

Mansa Musa died in 1332. He had ruled Mali for twenty-five years. His reign was so successful that some historians describe the history of western Africa in the 1300s as "the century of Musa." Mansa Musa's fame had spread beyond Africa's borders to Europe. European mapmakers began to include Mali on their maps.

Mali Declines

After Mansa Musa's death, his son Mansa Maghan (/mah*gan/) succeeded to the throne. Mansa Maghan ruled for only four years, but his reign was a disaster. First, Mali lost the city of Timbuktu. Second, Mansa Maghan allowed the two Songhai princes to escape. The princes established a new government that would become the Songhai Empire.

As you will discover in the next chapter, the growing threat of the Songhai Empire eventually proved too much for Mali. By 1500, Mali had lost its hold on the gold and salt trade across the Sahara. In the late 1400s, the Songhai Empire replaced Mali as the richest and most powerful empire in West Africa. And two captive princes made this happen.

Chapter 7
Songhai and Askia Muhammad

The Big Question

As Askia Muhammad expanded his empire, how did Islam grow within it?

Prisoners of War The two Songhai princes were named Ali Kolon and Sulyaman Nar. Ali Kolon was a fierce warrior and a natural leader. Mansa Musa had even had him lead military expeditions for Mali.

But Ali Kolon had some big plans of his own. According to legend, he cleverly used his military expeditions to plan his escape from Mali. On each military expedition for Mansa Musa, Ali Kolon got a little closer to his home in Gao. At every stop, he hid weapons and food in secret places that only he knew.

Mansa Maghan, who had gained the throne after his father's death, was a weak leader. This gave Ali Kolon the chance he had been waiting for during his seven years in Mali.

This terracotta horse and rider signify the wealth and power of the Mali Empire.

The Great Escape

Along with his brother and a few loyal supporters, Ali Kolon escaped from Niani, Mali's capital.

Ali Kolon became the new chief of Gao, the capital of the Songhai people. He started the Sonni (/soon*nee/) **Dynasty**. For most of the 1300s and during the early part of the 1400s, Mali and Songhai tried to overpower each other. Neither side had much luck. However, in 1464, the fierce Songhai king Sonni Ali Ber (/soo*nee/ahl*ee/bar/) came to the throne.

Hard Times for Timbuktu

In the early 1400s, nomads from the desert had invaded Timbuktu. Led by Chief Akil (/ah*keel/), the nomads decided not to live in the city they had conquered. Instead, they lived in the desert. They appointed allied representatives to collect taxes on behalf of Chief Akil. Also, Tuareg raids threatened the prosperous trade of the city. The residents of Timbuktu hoped that Sonni Ali Ber could bring back peace, stability, and prosperity to the city.

Vocabulary

dynasty, n. a series of rulers who are all from the same family

sack, v. to destroy and steal things in a city or building, usually with an army

And so the leaders of Timbuktu sent a letter to Sonni Ali Ber. They offered to give Timbuktu to the Songhai chief if he would get rid of Chief Akil.

Sonni Ali Ber wanted to control this important trading town. In 1468, he sent an army into Timbuktu. His troops **sacked** Timbuktu

The Songhai Empire revolved around the Niger River.

and killed many people, including scholars, teachers, and students who lived there.

The Capture of Jenne

The powerful Songhai Empire grew stronger under Sonni Ali Ber. Then, about five years after he sacked Timbuktu, in 1473, Sonni Ali Ber conquered Jenne. Jenne was a city about three hundred miles southwest of Timbuktu. Like Timbuktu, Jenne was a great center of learning and trade on the Niger River.

Jenne was a hard city to capture. It was surrounded by swamps. So, Sonni Ali Ber started a **siege** of Jenne. For seven years, Sonni Ali Ber and his men cut off supplies

Vocabulary

siege, n. a battle strategy in which enemy soldiers surround a building or place so that those under attack cannot receive supplies

This painting shows an American artist's imagining of how Jenne looked centuries ago. Jenne is still an important market town on the Niger River.

This image shows the markets of Jenne today.

to Jenne. Finally, its citizens gave up. Sonni Ali Ber was impressed by the courage of the people of Jenne. Sonni Ali Ber decided to marry the **queen mother** of Jenne. The Songhai Empire became the main power in West Africa.

Sonni Ali Ber kept his huge empire firmly under his control by dividing his lands into smaller regions. He appointed a governor to rule each region.

Vocabulary

queen mother, n. the mother of the current king; often seen as a person with power in African kingdoms

social system, n. how a society is organized in terms of who is given power and respect

Life in the Songhai Empire

Songhai had a strict **social system**. At the top of the system were the descendants of the original Songhai people. They had special rights and lived apart from others.

The next level in Songhai was made up of traders, merchants, and soldiers. Trade and a strong army kept Songhai powerful. Unlike other armies in West Africa, the Songhai army was made of professional soldiers. Songhai's professional army was much more efficient and effective.

Then there were farmers and craftspeople. People did the jobs their families had done before them. If your family were weavers, then you became a weaver.

At the bottom of the Songhai social system were enslaved workers. Like many other societies, West Africans had been enslaving prisoners of war and criminals for years. Enslaved workers were often sold to other African kingdoms. Local enslaved workers kept some rights, including the right to buy their freedom and to marry.

Both Islam and traditional religions influenced life in Songhai. Throughout the 1400s, the Songhai kings somewhat followed the teachings of Islam. However, they were not very religious. Most people in Songhai shared their leader's attitude toward Islam. Some continued to worship their own traditional gods.

Askia Muhammad Rules

Sonni Ali Ber died in 1492. He had ruled for twenty-eight years. The Muslims in Songhai refused to accept his son, Sonni Baru, as king. Like his father, Sonni Baru did not follow Islam closely. Askia Muhammad Toure, one of the king's soldiers, was also unhappy. Unlike the rulers of the Sonni dynasty, Askia Muhammad was a very **devout** Muslim. He led a revolt against the new king.

> **Vocabulary**
>
> **devout,** adj. showing deep religious feelings

In 1493, Askia Muhammad's army defeated the king. He established the Askia dynasty, which was named after him.

The Muslims of Songhai celebrated their new leader and his deep faith in Islam. With Askia Muhammad in control of the government, Muslim scholars, teachers, and students once again settled in Timbuktu. They knew they would be safe from religious persecution. Askia Muhammad respected their vast learning. He protected them and asked them for advice.

The Songhai Empire Expands

As other rulers before him had done, Askia Muhammad began to expand his empire. In the west, he took land that had belonged to Mali. He also conquered lands to the south of Songhai. Askia Muhammad took many prisoners. Many of these prisoners were children who became soldiers in his army. Around 1513, Askia Muhammad's soldiers invaded the lands of the Hausa people east of the Niger River. Though he exercised little control over the Hausa, all of Askia Muhammad's conquests created a huge, tightly knit empire.

Askia Muhammad's Pilgrimage

Askia Muhammad knew that it was his duty to make a trip to Mecca. So in 1495, he set off to Mecca on a two-year pilgrimage. As you would expect, his caravan was huge. About five hundred horsemen and one thousand soldiers accompanied the king. He also took a great deal of gold, reported to be 300,000 "pieces." About a third of the gold went to charity. Another third paid his traveling expenses. The remaining third paid for wonderful souvenirs. He also bought buildings so that other West African Muslims who were making the pilgrimage could find places to stay.

But Askia Muhammad didn't travel to Mecca just to give charity and buy beautiful things. Far from it. As a serious Muslim, he tried to set an example for all Muslims through his faith and worship. Askia Muhammad saw it as his **sacred** duty to spread Islam all through West Africa.

Vocabulary

sacred, adj. related to religion; holy

As his empire enlarged, Askia Muhammad appointed Muslim judges in every district. These judges used Muslim justice in place of traditional Songhai laws. His own court followed the same religious guidelines. As a result of these measures, Islam spread throughout West Africa.

Askia Muhammad's final years were difficult. One of his own sons overthrew him. He exiled Askia Muhammad to a lonely, miserable

Askia Muhammad's tomb is an important historical site in the country of Mali today.

island. Finally, in his last years, Askia Muhammad was allowed to return home. He died in 1538.

The Songhai Empire continued to thrive until the late 1500s. In that time North Africans began to invade the empire. The empire was also under attack from the south, as slave traders raided villages. Captured people were traded to Europeans and sent to the Americas. By the 1700s, the Songhai Empire had shrunk to the area around Gao.

Chapter 8
The Travels of Ibn Battuta

> **The Big Question**
>
> Why were the travels of Ibn Batutta so extraordinary for the time in which he lived?

See the World Today, airplanes, trains, cars, and buses make it easy to travel to faraway places. However, this was not always the case. In medieval times, travel was dangerous and difficult. Very few people traveled far from their villages. Ibn Battuta was a remarkable exception.

Ibn Battuta traveled far and wide throughout the Muslim world. Fortunately, he wrote all about his journeys. His writings give readers a peek into the world of medieval Islam.

Ibn Battuta was born in 1304 in Tangiers, Morocco. He was a world traveler, writer, and geographer. By the end of his life in 1368, he had journeyed across Africa, Arabia, Turkey, India, and China. He is the only traveler we know about who visited all the major Muslim-ruled countries in the 1300s. Scholars estimate that he traveled up to 75,000 miles.

This early map shows how little was known about the world in the time of Ibn Battuta.

It All Started with a Pilgrimage

As a child, Ibn Battuta probably never imagined that he would become the most famous traveler of his day. Because he was a very religious Muslim, Ibn Battuta hoped to visit Mecca, the Muslim holy city.

Ibn Battuta stopped in Cairo on his way to Mecca.

He was lucky to be able to make the holy pilgrimage. Ibn Battuta came from a wealthy, educated Muslim family who could afford the journey. Because of his family, Ibn Battuta would have received a good education. He would have studied the Koran and learned about Islamic law.

When he was twenty-one years old, Ibn Battuta went on a pilgrimage, traveling east from Tangier, Morocco, across northern Africa. Later that same year, Ibn Battuta reached Egypt, the first stop on his pilgrimage to Mecca. Next, he traveled to Damascus in Syria. There he joined some other Muslim pilgrims headed for Mecca. This journey sparked Ibn Battuta's interest in seeing more of the world. He decided he would visit other Muslim regions in the world.

Traveling Man

Ibn Battuta spent three years in Mecca. In addition to completing his religious obligations as a Muslim by making his *hajj*, Ibn Battuta also studied Islamic law. When he completed his studies, Ibn Battuta qualified as a Muslim judge.

Then Ibn Battuta began traveling again. His fellow Muslims often gave him food and places to stay all along his route. First, he traveled down the coast of East Africa, stopping at the Swahili trading cities of Mombasa and Kilwa. Then he traveled across the Black Sea, stopping first to visit Constantinople. He then traveled across the **steppe** of central Asia. Finally, he arrived in India. The **sultan** there made Ibn Battuta a judge of the city of Delhi. Later, the sultan

Vocabulary

steppe, n. grassland plain

sultan, n. a king or ruler of a Muslim country

Ibn Battuta spent several years as an Islamic judge in the Maldives.

even asked Ibn Battuta to lead a group of Indians on a visit to the emperor of China.

Ibn Batutta's trip was going very well until a storm hit. He ended up in southeastern India without any money. Fortunately, he was able to sail to the Maldives, a group of islands off the southern coast of India. There, he got a job as a judge. But Ibn Battuta still wanted to see the world. In 1345, he voyaged to what is today called Sri Lanka. After his visit there, he resumed his trip to China. He landed in China at the port city of Zaytun (now called Ch'üan-chou) in southeastern China. He later traveled as far inland as Beijing.

Later, on his way back to Morocco, he stopped at Sumatra, Malabar, Oman, Baghdad, Cairo, and Tunis. In 1349, Ibn Battuta arrived home in Morocco.

But Ibn Battuta's travels were not over. Instead, he traveled to the city of Granada in Spain. After two years in Spain, he traveled to the Mali Empire in 1352.

Ibn Battuta trekked by camel caravan across the Sahara. He visited the people who lived along the Niger River in West Africa. Ibn Battuta trudged along the trade routes that you read about in previous chapters. He stayed for months at a time with chiefs in the territories of the great empire of Mali. He even visited and stayed in Timbuktu and Gao, and with the nomads who camped along the Niger River.

Ibn Battuta's Travel Book

Ibn Battuta's extraordinary travels made him famous in his own day. But because he wrote down his adventures, he is still famous today.

Ibn Battuta's travel book contains colorful details and descriptions. Battuta visited Mali at the height of that empire's power. For example, in his book he describes seeing a sultan appearing in his palace garden. He carried a bow and a quiver of arrows. The sultan wore a gold cap and a red velvet **tunic**. The sultan was surrounded by musicians who played gold and silver instruments.

Vocabulary

tunic, n. a long shirt that extends below the hips, often to the knees

Ibn Battuta called his book *Rihlah*, which means the journey. A fitting name, indeed! Scholars still consider *Rihlah* a reliable source of information about the medieval Islamic world.

Ibn Battuta's Travels

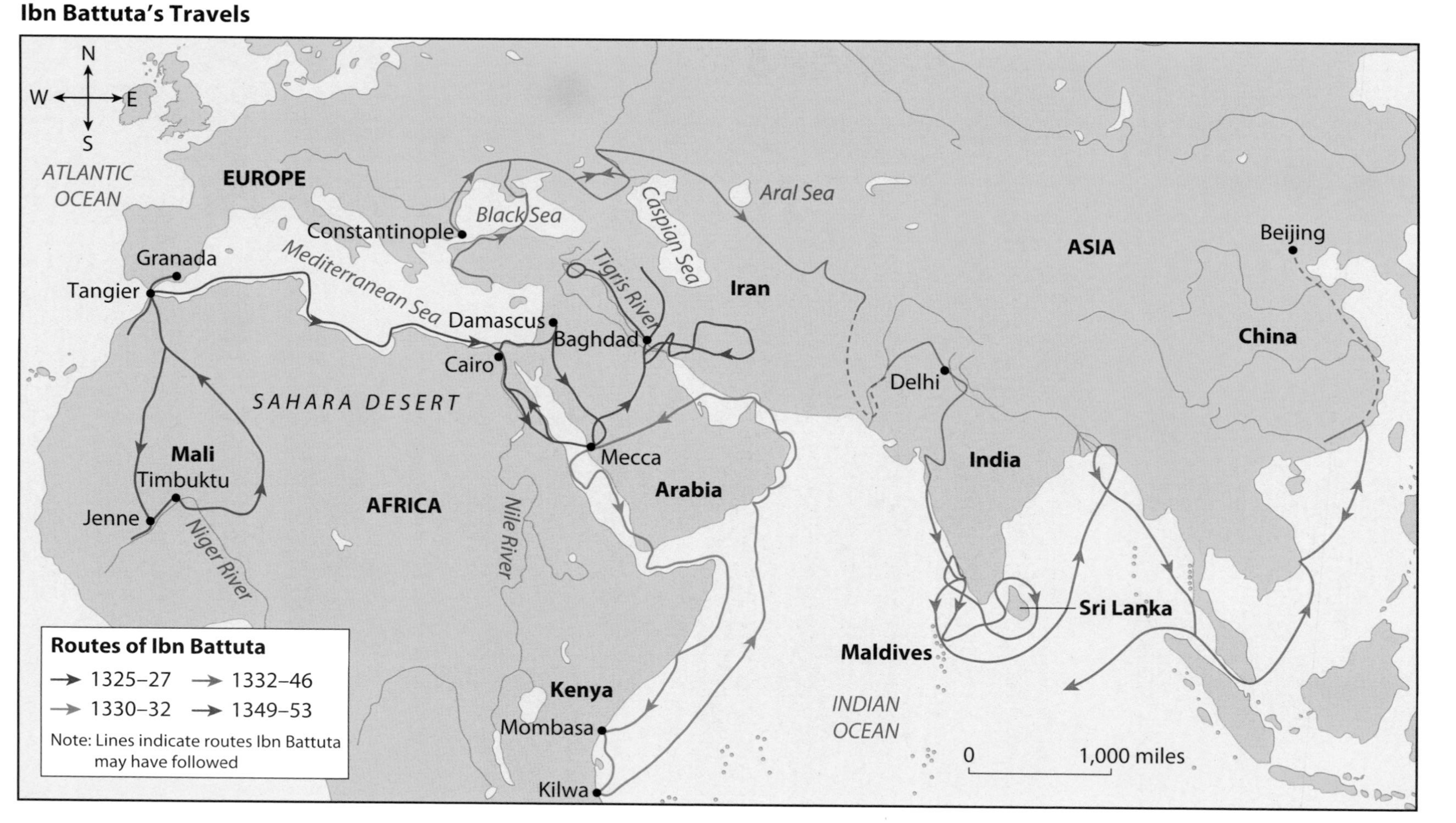

The Traveler of Islam

Ibn Battuta's extensive journeys to Muslim countries earned him the nickname "the Traveler of Islam." He claimed to have met sixty rulers and thousands of people during his travels. Along the way, Ibn Battuta rode in a dog sled, sailed on a Chinese ship called a junk, and crossed the Atlas Mountains in northern Africa during a blizzard.

After his last journey, Ibn Battuta returned home where he spent his last days. He died in about 1368.

In 1829, an English scholar discovered Ibn Battuta's book and translated it into English. Ibn Battuta's name and adventures spread to new generations of readers. People celebrated his bravery, intelligence, and courage. Modern scientists even named a **crater** on the moon after him.

Vocabulary

crater, n. a large hole in the ground made by an explosion or something falling out of the sky

Atlas

Kingdoms and Physical Geography of Africa

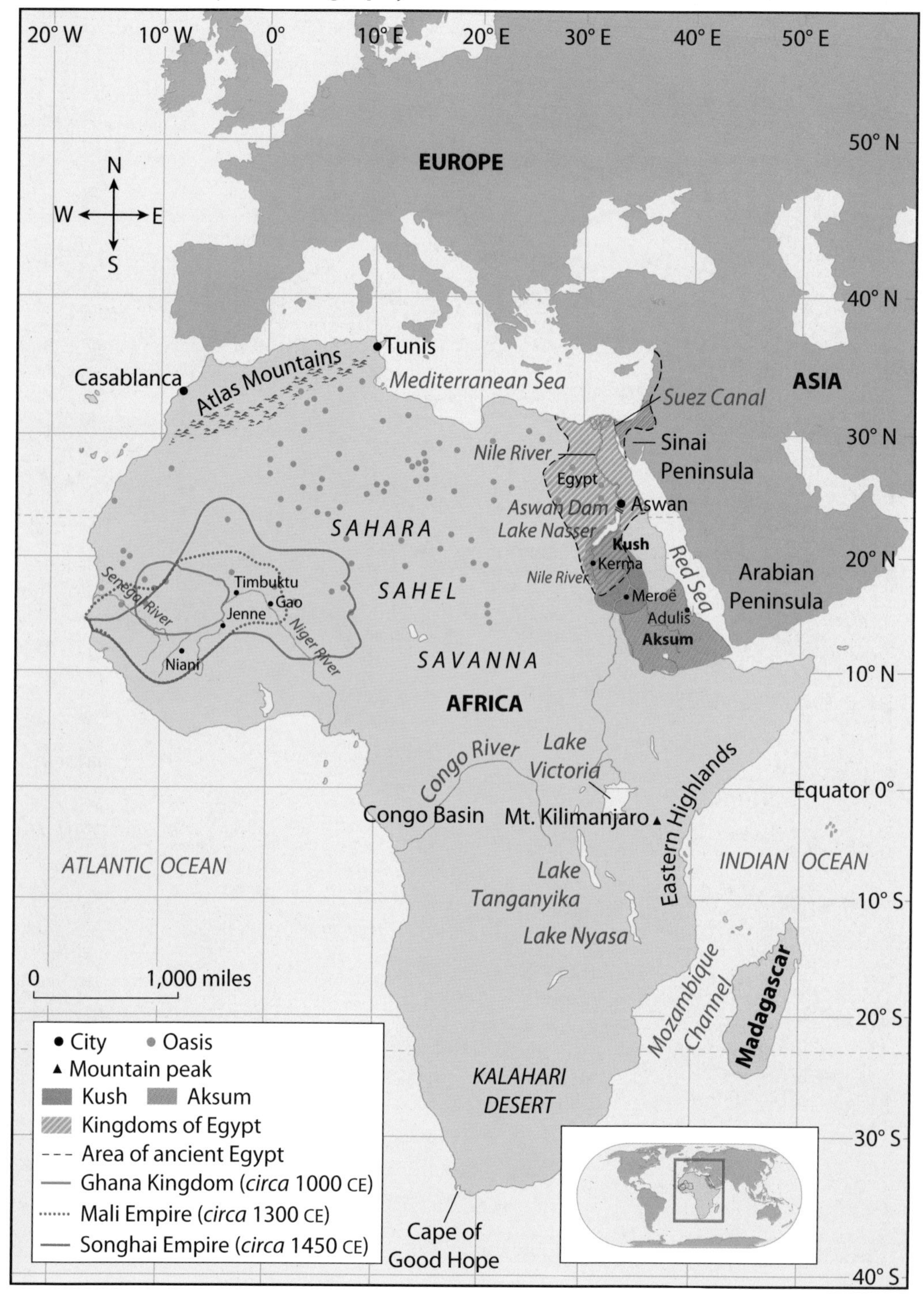

Physical Geography of Africa

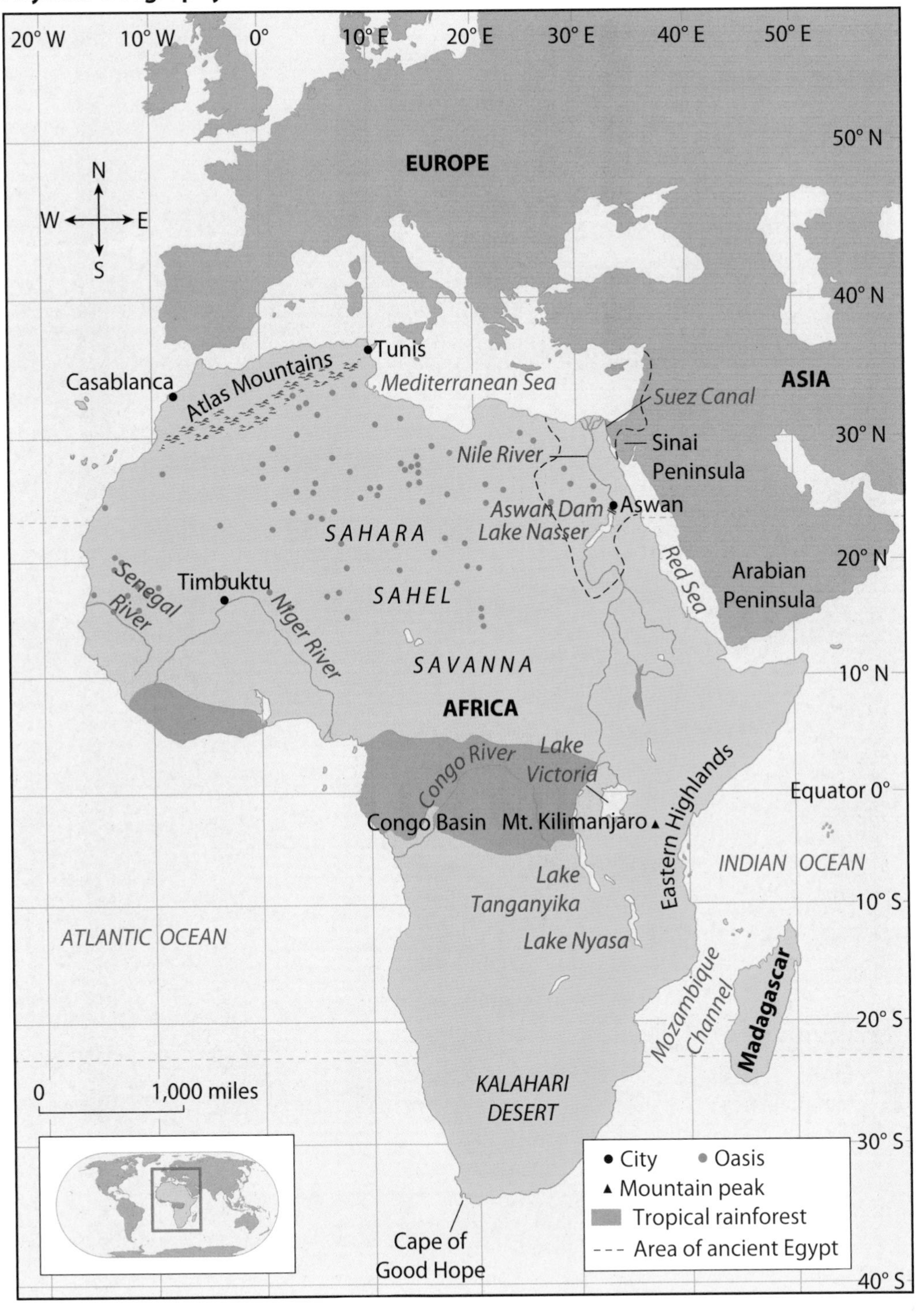

Glossary

A

archaeologist, n. an expert in the study of ancient people and the objects from their time period that remain **(62)**

artifact, n. an object used during a past period in history **(62)**

C

cape, n. a point of land extending into water **(50)**

captive, n. a prisoner **(88)**

caravan, n. a group of travelers journeying together, often across a desert **(66)**

cowrie shell, n. a type of shell found in the Indian and Pacific oceans that was used as money in some cultures **(69)**

crater, n. a large hole in the ground made by an explosion or something falling out of the sky **(107)**

D

devout, adj. showing deep religious feelings **(96)**

dynasty, n. a series of rulers who are all from the same family **(92)**

E

ebony wood, n. a dark, hard wood that comes from tropical trees **(60)**

empire, n. a group of countries controlled by a single authority **(56)**

G

goods, n. items that people want to buy **(58)**

I

incense, n. something that has a pleasant smell when it is burned **(60)**

K

kingdom, n. a country ruled by a king or queen **(56)**

kola nut, n. the fruit of the kola tree found in tropical regions of Africa **(70)**

L

lavish, adj. rich or expensive **(87)**

legend, n. an old, well-known story that is usually more entertaining than truthful **(81)**

M

Mandinka, n. the group of people living in West Africa who ruled the Mali Empire **(80)**

mansa, n. the title used by kings in the Mali Empire **(82)**

mosque, n. a place of worship for Muslims **(68)**

N

natural resource, n. something from nature that is useful to humans **(58)**

nomadic, adj. moving around, often in search of food; not settled in one place **(53)**

O

oasis, n. an area in the desert where there are water and plants **(52)**

P

pilgrimage, n. a journey undertaken for a religious purpose **(86)**

Q

quarry, n. a place where stone or minerals are taken from the earth (68)

queen mother, n. the mother of the current king; often seen as a person with power in African kingdoms (95)

quill, n. the central part of a bird's feather, often used as a tool for writing (75)

R

ravine, n. a small, deep, narrow valley (53)

S

sack, v. to destroy and steal things in a city or building, usually with an army (92)

sacred, adj. related to religion; holy (97)

siege, n. a battle strategy in which enemy soldiers surround a building or place so that those under attack cannot receive supplies (93)

social system, n. how a society is organized in terms of who is given power and respect (95)

sorghum, n. a type of grain fed to animals; also used for making a type of porridge for people to eat (54)

splay, v. to spread out (68)

steppe, n. grassland plain (103)

sultan, n. a king or ruler of a Muslim country (103)

T

tax, n. money that people are required to pay to support the workings of the government (74)

tunic, n. a long shirt that extends below the hips, often to the knees (105)

U

university, n. a school where advanced learning is taught (83)

CKHG™

Core Knowledge History and Geography™

Series Editor-in-Chief

E. D. Hirsch, Jr.

Medieval Islamic Empires

Subject Matter Expert

Ahmed H. al-Rahim, PhD, Department of Religious Studies, University of Virginia

Illustration and Photo Credits

Cover Images: Muslim physician, Preparation of medicines for the treatment of patient suffering from smallpox, miniature from the Canon of medicine, by Avicenna (980-1037), Ottoman manuscript, Turkey,17th century / De Agostini Picture Library / G. Dagli Orti / Bridgeman Images; Minaret of a mosque, Wolfgang Kaehler / SuperStock

DeAgostini/Superstock: 22

Egypt - Syria: Portrait of Saladin (Salah al-Din Yusuf ibn Ayyub, 1138–1193), Abu al-'Iz Ibn Isma'il ibn al-Razaz al-Jazari (1136–1206), 15th century. Although Al-Jazari was a contemporary of Saladin, the attribution remains disputed / Pictures from History / Bridgeman Images: 39

Fr 9084 f.20v: Departure for the First Crusade (vellum), William of Tyre (Archbishop) (c.1130–85) / Bibliotheque Nationale, Paris, France / Bridgeman Images: 36

Godong/robertharding/Superstock: 10

IberfotoSuperstock: 24

Mecca surrounded by the Mountains of Arafa (gouache on paper), Islamic School, (19th century) / Popular Traditions Museum, Damascus, Syria / Bridgeman Images: 19

Middle East: The destruction of the idols at the Kaaba in Mecca by the Prophet Muhammad, as envisaged in 'L'Histoire Merveilleuse en Vers de Mahomet', 16th or 17th-century) / Pictures from History / Bridgeman Images: 20

MS 447 View of Medina and mosque of the Prophet Muhammad (opaque pigments on paper), Ottoman School, (18th century) / © The Trustees of the Chester Beatty Library, Dublin / Bridgeman Images: 17

Pope Urban II announcing First Crusade, 1095, miniature taken from This history of Crusades by Guillaume de Tyr, 15th century French manuscript, History of Crusades, 11th century / De Agostini Picture Library / Bridgeman Images: 34–35

Preparation of medicines for the treatment of patient suffering from smallpox,miniature from the Canon of medicine,by Avicenna (980–1037),Ottoman manuscript,Turkey,17th century / De Agostini Picture Library / G. Dagli Orti / Bridgeman Images: 1, 30

Richard Coeur de Lion on his way to Jerusalem, Glass, James William (1825–57) / Private Collection / Photo © Bonhams, London, UK / Bridgeman Images: 40

Robert Huberman/Superstock: 32

robertharding/Superstock: 12–13, 28, 29

The Archangel Gabriel inspiring Mohammed in the mosque of medina (gouache on paper), Ottoman School, (18th century) / Museum of Turkish and Islamic Art, Istanbul, Turkey / Photo © AISA / Bridgeman Images: 7

The faithful before the Kaaba in Mecca, from the 'Siyer-i Nebi' (gouache on paper), Turkish School, (16th century)/Topkapi Palace Museum, Istanbul, Turkey / Bildarchiv Steffens / Bridgeman Images: 14

Travel Library Limited/Superstock: i, iii, 3

Travel Pictures Ltd/Superstock: 31

Troops of Sultan Mohammed II laying siege to Constantinople in 1453 (vellum), Ottoman School, (15th century) / Bibliotheque Nationale, Paris, France / De Agostini Picture Library / Bridgeman Images: 42

View of Mosul (From the Tigris). Baghdad, The Capital of Iraq, Stands On the Banks of the Tigris. / Private Collection / Photo © Liszt Collection / Bridgeman Images: 26–27

Wolfgang Kaehler/Superstock: 5

Early and Medieval African Kingdoms

Subject Matter Expert

David Owusu-Ansah, PhD, Department of History, James Madison University

Illustration and Photo Credits

Cover Images: Gold jewelry, Pectoral, from Senegal, 13th-18th century (gold), African School / Musee de l'Institut Francais d'Afrique Noire, Dakar, Senegal / Bridgeman Images; Mansa Musa, Mansa Kankan Musa I, 14th century king of the Mali empire (gouache on paper), McBride, Angus (1931-2007) / Private Collection / © Look and Learn / Bridgeman Images; Kushite pyramids, John Warburton Lee/SuperStock A Camel Train, 1899 (panel), Lazerges, Paul John Baptiste (1845-1902) / Private Collection / Photo © Bonhams, London, UK / Bridgeman Images: 66–67

age fotostock/SuperStock: 72–73

An aerial view of the islands of Maldives (photo) / Majority World/UIG / Bridgeman Images: 104

Canoes on the Niger River (engraving), English School, (19th century) / Private Collection / Bridgeman Images: 93

Coptic cross, Axum, Tigray, Ethiopia / De Agostini Picture Library / N. Cirani / Bridgeman Images: 64

Detail from the Catalan Atlas, 1375 (vellum), Cresques, Abraham (1325–87) / Bibliotheque Nationale, Paris, France / Bridgeman Images: 45, 84–85

Early Egyptians using a system of weights and poles called shadoofs to get water from the Nile, Jackson, Peter (1922–2003) / Private Collection / © Look and Learn / Bridgeman Images: 57

Gold bracelet of Queen Amanishakheto. Meroe. Egypt. / Neues Museum, Berlin, Germany / Photo © Tarker / Bridgeman Images: 62

Horse and Rider, Djenne, Mali (terracotta), African School / Private Collection / Photo © Heini Schneebeli / Bridgeman Images: 91

Iberfoto/SuperStock: 100–101

Jeremy Woodhouse/Blend Images/SuperStock: 53

John Warburton Lee/SuperStock: 61, 88, 94

JTB Photo/SuperStock: 51

Kirina, one of the three Malinke towns that formed the foundation of Sundiata's empire of Mali / Werner Forman Archive / Bridgeman Images: 78–79

Mansa Kankan Musa I, 14th century king of the Mali empire (gouache on paper), McBride, Angus (1931–2007) / Private Collection / © Look and Learn / Bridgeman Images: 87

Map of North Africa and West Africa, published in Strasbourg in 1522 (coloured engraving), Ptolemy (Claudius Ptolemaeus of Alexandria)(c.90–168)(after) / Bibliotheque des Arts Decoratifs, Paris, France / Archives Charmet / Bridgeman Images: 46–47

Minden Pictures/SuperStock: 69

National Geographic/SuperStock: 55

Pectoral, from Senegal, 13th-18th century (gold), African School / Musee de l'Institut Francais d'Afrique Noire, Dakar, Senegal / Bridgeman Images: 74

Peter Giovannini/imageBROKER/SuperStock: 71

Pilgrims on Mount Arafa on the 9th day of Dhul-Hijjah, 1918 (colour litho), Dinet, Alphonse Etienne (1861–1929) / Private Collection / Archives Charmet / Bridgeman Images: 86

Salt from the Sahara for sale (photo) / Insights/UIG / Bridgeman Images: 76

Shari Darley Griffiths: 58–59

The Great mosque at Djenne, Mali / Werner Forman Archive / Bridgeman Images: 82

The Great Pyramid of Giizeh, English School, (20th century) / Private Collection / © Look and Learn / Bridgeman Images: 102

The markets in Jenne-jeno c.1000 AD (colour litho), Santore, Charles (b.1935) / National Geographic Creative / Bridgeman Images: 94

The North Side of Timbuktoo, from 'Les Voyages en Afrique' by Heinrich Barth published in 1857, (colour litho), Bernatz, Johann Martin (1802–1878) (after) / Bibliotheque Nationale, Paris, France / Archives Charmet / Bridgeman Images: 83

The tomb of Askia Mohammed, ruler of the Songhai empire from 1493 to 1528, at Gao / Werner Forman Archive / Bridgeman Images: 98

Wolfgang Kaehler/SuperStock: 45, 88